SOVEREIGN LIVING I

THE
SOVEREIGN METHOD

REFLECT · REFRAME · RECONNECT
A GUIDED JOURNAL
TO RECLAIM YOUR CROWN

LAURA ALFANO

Sovereign Living I The Sovereign Method:
Reflect • Reframe • Reconnect
A Guided Journal to Reclaim Your Crown

Laura Alfano

Laura Alfano
Alfano, Inc.
Malibu, California
LauraAlfano22@gmail.com
LauraAlfano.com

ISBN – 979-8-9938449-3-0

First Edition
10 9 8 7 6 5 4 3 2 1

Printed in the United States of America

SOVEREIGN LIVING I

THE
SOVEREIGN METHOD

REFLECT · REFRAME · RECONNECT
A GUIDED JOURNAL
TO RECLAIM YOUR CROWN

CONTENT

PART THREE - MANIFESTATION **129**

AUTHOR'S NOTE

Dearest Reader,

This guided journal is an invitation to go beyond reading and into embodiment. *Sovereign Living* is not simply meant to be understood, it is meant to be lived. These pages are where your transformation becomes personal, where insight becomes action, and where your voice meets your truth.

Within each section, you will be guided through The Sovereign Method: **Reflect, Reframe, and Reconnect**. This practice is designed to gently illuminate where you may be giving your power away, support you in shifting your perspective with compassion and clarity, and guide you back into alignment with your inner authority.

Reflect invites honest awareness. It is where you pause, look inward, and name what is true for you without judgment.

Reframe opens the door to possibility. Here, you soften old narratives, release limiting beliefs, and choose a more empowered perspective.

Reconnect brings you home to yourself. Through intention, intuition, and aligned action, you anchor into the woman you are becoming.

This guided journal is not about getting it "right." It is about being real. Write freely. Be honest. Let these pages hold what you may not have yet spoken out loud. There is no timeline, no perfection, only a steady return to yourself.

The journey of *Sovereign Living* is one of remembering. Everything you are seeking already lives within you. These exercises are here to help you access it, trust it, and live from it.

Take your time. Move at your own pace. This is your space to reclaim your Crown.

Welcome back to yourself,

Laura

Part One

RECOGNITION

CHOOSING LOVE, HEALING
FEAR & AWAKENING WISDOM

CRISIS TO WILLFUL CHANGE

"A crisis exists for you
to have victory over it."
~ *Guru Jagat*

From Crisis to Courageous Change

Crisis alone does not create transformation. Instead, crisis offers you a choice. You can collapse back into the old, or rise into the new. Making the correct choice requires self-awareness, intention, and courage to hear the inner voice that already knows the way.

To emerge victorious in a crisis:

- Pause. When shock hits, breathe. Give your nervous system time to settle.

- Zoom out. Look at the big picture. Break it down into manageable steps. What needs your attention in the next few hours? The next few days?

____

____

____

____

____

____

____

____

- Stay calm. Whether you're navigating loss, heartbreak, or sudden change, remind yourself: You are still here. You will be okay.

- Reach out. Don't isolate yourself. Call your support system. Let people witness and support you.

- Seek guidance that helps you see with new eyes, whether legal, financial, or emotional, and walk beside wisdom as you navigate the path ahead.

- Take accountability. Where were the signs? Did you override your intuition? Be honest with yourself without blaming yourself.

____

____

____

____

- Feel the emotions. Don't numb or bypass them. Let the pain rise, feel it, observe it and release it.

- Begin again. When you're ready, shift your focus toward healing, reinvention, and take actions that align with victory.

Recognizing Crisis Before It Hits

Your intuition of a crisis is like a traffic light:

- Green Light (Whisper): A soft inner voice says, "Something feels off." You ignore it and keep going without paying much attention to the warning from your intuition.

- Yellow Light (Tap): The discomfort grows. You feel tension. Doubt creeps in. You slow down, think more about it, and just keep going.

- Red Light (Crash): You ignored the whispers. You ignored the taps. Either you full stop or life hits the breaks for you.

This is the moment of reckoning, and your greatest opportunity. You can crash again, or you can course-correct, heal, and grow.

So sit with the pain. Listen to what it's asking of you. Let it shape you into someone wiser, deeper, and more free.

Reflect

Awareness is the first tool for transformation. By looking back without judgment, you prepare to move forward with intention.

- Recall your last personal crisis. What triggered it and how did you react emotionally, physically, or spiritually?

____

____

____

____

____

____

- Were there signs beforehand? Did your body, intuition, or environment try to warn you?

____

____

____

- What wisdom emerged through that experience? Did it reveal any patterns, boundary breaches, or outdated coping strategies?

____

____

____

Journaling Prompt: *What was my most recent crisis trying to show me? What signals did I miss, and how can I listen more closely next time?*

____

____

____

____

Reframe

Crisis may feel like collapse, but it often clears the path for deeper alignment. When we choose to see through the lens of growth, we reclaim our power.

- A crisis is not the end; it's a threshold. A chance to realign your life with what's true and needed.

- Your breakdown could be the soil where your next breakthrough takes root.

- Crisis strips away illusion. It doesn't arrive to punish you, but to wake you up and bring you closer to wholeness.

Journal Prompt: *Instead of asking "Why is this happening to me?" Try: "What is this trying to wake up in me?"*

____

____

____

____

Reconnect

After a storm, you rebuild by returning to what's real: your values, your vision, your voice. This is where healing takes root.

- Reconnect with your inner wisdom. In stillness or reflection, ask: "What does my soul need most right now?"

____

____

____

____

- Ground yourself in simple truths: people, practices, or places that bring strength, peace, or perspective.

- Begin shaping your post-crisis vision. What will you no longer tolerate? What new boundaries or commitments will you honor moving forward?

____

____

____

____

Affirmation: *I trust that this moment is shaping me, not breaking me. I choose growth, clarity, and willful change.*

Notes:

____

____

____

____

____

____

____

____

____

____

FEAR TO LOVE

How to Choose Love over Fear

To choose love over fear is to return to your natural state of wholeness. Fear contracts; love expands. Fear builds walls; love opens doors. Choosing love is not a single act but a daily practice, a conscious decision to respond with compassion instead of control, curiosity instead of judgment, and trust instead of doubt. When you meet life's challenges through the lens of love, you no longer seek safety in certainty but in self-awareness. Love becomes both your compass and your guide, leading you back to peace, power, and truth.

Reflect

Shifting from fear to love is not a one-time decision but a daily devotion to healing, choosing, and returning home to who you really are.

- Fear often hides in plain sight, disguised as control, anxiety, avoidance, or self-doubt. The first step is bringing it into the light.

- Identify the fears currently driving your choices. Are you acting from love, or protecting yourself from loss, rejection, or failure?

____

____

____

____

- What fears are in charge of your life right now?

____

____

- Where did they begin?

____

____

- What younger part of you is still fearful and still trying to stay safe?

____

____

- Reflect on your emotional memory. When was the last time fear influenced your feelings?

____

____

- How did that affect the outcome?

____

____

Journaling Prompt: *Where in my life am I ready to release fear and return to love? What would choosing my truth look like here?*

____

____

____

____

Reframe

Fear is loud, but love is wise. You don't have to silence fear, you just have to stop letting it lead.

- Fear is not your identity; it's a protective belief system built from past pain. It served you once, but you've outgrown it.

- Choosing love doesn't mean you'll never feel afraid again. It means choosing trust, presence and compassion over fear.

- Even small acts of love toward yourself, others, or the world can interrupt fear and rewire your nervous system toward safety and peace.

Mantra: *Fear may visit, but love leads. When I feel fear, I am safe to choose love again.*

Reconnect

Returning to love is a practice, one of remembering, re-centering, and reparenting the parts of you that learned fear too early.

- See beauty first. Wear rose-colored glasses not to deny reality, but to train your mind to look for love before fear.

- Hand over your fear. You don't have to carry it anymore. Offer it to God, the universe, or your higher self and breathe.

- When in doubt, consult your inner child. Ask: "What would I tell my six-year-old self right now?" Then act on the most loving answer.

____

____

____

____

Affirmation: *I am no longer led by fear. I trust the voice of love within me to guide me, to protect me, and to restore me.*

Notes:

____

____

____

____

____

____

____

____

____

____

____

HEAD TO HEART

How to Tap into Your Heart Before Your Ego

The ego wants to protect, defend, and control. The heart wants to connect, heal, and expand. In moments of tension, distance, or indecision, the key is not to silence the ego, but to let the heart speak first. This practice helps you soften, listen inward, and lead with love.

Reflect

Begin by noticing when your mind has been louder than your heart, and how that has shaped your choices.

- Is there someone you love but have distanced yourself from because of pride, fear, or self-protection?

____

____

____

____

- Where in your life are you stuck in your head, overthinking, overanalyzing, or second-guessing?

____

____

____

- Recall a moment when you ignored your intuition. What was the cost?

____

____

____

Journaling Prompt: *Where have I let ego lead instead of my heart? What would shift if I allowed my heart to go first, even if it feels vulnerable?*

____

____

____

____

____

____

____

____

Reframe

Your heart is deeply wise. Choosing your heart doesn't mean erasing boundaries; it means aligning with your deeper truth.

- Reaching out doesn't erase what happened, but it creates space for a new future to emerge.

- The ego seeks control, but the heart seeks truth and healing.

- Vulnerability is not a weakness. It's the bravest doorway to authentic connection.

Mantra: *My heart knows the way; fear steps aside. My boundaries protect my truth, not my walls. Each act of vulnerability opens the way for healing, connection, and a future built on love.*

Reconnect

Connection begins with a softening, a willingness to return to love, even if you were once hurt. Let your healing ripple outward.

- What would love do right now, if it were leading this moment?

____

____

____

____

- If there's a relationship in need of repair, take one gentle step: a message, a call, or an honest conversation.

- Soften. Speak from your heart, not your wounds. Let the other person feel seen, not judged.

- During my own healing, I practiced the *Sopurkh* mantra, a sacred chant for divine masculine healing. I visualized my son, my brother and my father. The sound softened my heart and restored peace from within.

Affirmation: *I lead with love, not fear. My heart is my guide, my strength, and my home.*

Notes:

____

____

____

____

____

____

____

____

____

____

____

SEPARATION TO ONE

"We are all one.
Only egos, beliefs and
fears separate us."
~ Nikola Tesla

How to Connect as ONE from Separation

Separation is often invisible, built through small judgments, conditioned fears, or a sense of "us versus them." But when we remember that we belong to one another, walls soften. Connection doesn't require agreement; it requires humanity. This practice invites you to shift from division to unity, from protection to presence.

Reflect

Connection begins with awareness. Where have you built walls instead of bridges, intentionally or unconsciously?

____

____

____

____

____

____

____

____

- Reflect on people or groups you may have "othered" based on behavior, beliefs, or background. What stories did you create about them?

____

____

____

____

- Where do you notice separation showing up in your world, in your community, your relationships, or even your thoughts?

____

____

____

____

- Recall a time when someone extended compassion or understanding toward you when you didn't expect it. What impact did that have?

____

____

____

____

Journaling Prompt: *Where have I created distance when I could have offered curiosity or compassion?*

____

____

____

____

How might I begin to see others, especially those I struggle with, as part of the same human family?

____

____

____

____

Reframe

When we remember that every person carries a story, compassion becomes natural. Separation loses power when we choose to see with the heart.

- The unhoused person is not a statistic. He or she is someone's child, someone's story.

- A difficult co-worker may be fighting battles you can't see. You don't need to fix everyone, but recognize their humanity.

- People you disagree with aren't your enemy. They are on a different path. They are not a different worth.

Mantra: *I release the illusion of separation. I choose to see others as part of me, worthy, whole, and human.*

Reconnect

Bridge the gap with small, intentional acts of kindness. Love isn't loud; it's consistent, compassionate, and creative.

- Perform one quiet act of kindness today. Not for recognition, but as a gesture of unity. Let it ripple.

- Leave behind something uplifting: a note, a book, a compliment, or a care package. Let someone feel seen.

- Reach out to someone grieving, struggling, or overlooked. A simple, sincere message can remind them: *You're not alone.*

Affirmation: *I am connected to every soul I meet. My kindness is a thread that weaves the world back together.*

Notes:

____

____

____

____

____

____

____

____

____

____

____

____

SERVE OTHERS TO SERVING SELF, FIRST

"In case of a cabin pressure emergency, put on your own mask first before assisting others."
~ Every airline flight attendant, every flight

How Do We Nourish Ourselves Before Others?

It starts by listening to yourself, not just to others. It means remembering that your dreams matter. That your needs are valid. You're not only in service to others' needs. You're in service to your own.

Nourishing yourself isn't a retreat from love, it's a return to it. When you meet your own needs with compassion and intention, you can show up for others with authenticity, energy, and grace. Self-nourishment is the root of sustainable giving.

Reflect

Before you can refill your cup, you must see where it's leaking:

- Have you been living to meet others' expectations, while your own desires sit quietly in the background?

____

____

____

____

- What part of your life feels overextended or ignored, your body, your spirit, your time, your dreams?

____

____

____

____

- When was the last time you said "yes" out of obligation, even though your body or heart was saying "no"?

____

____

____

____

Journaling Prompt: *Where in my life am I abandoning my own needs in order to meet someone else's?*

____

____

____

____

What would it look like to turn some of that care inward, starting today?

____

____

____

Reframe

Self-prioritization is not a betrayal of love; it's the foundation of it. You lead with greater impact when you're rooted in self-awareness.

- Self-care is not self-indulgent. It's essential. You are the vessel through which your love flows.

- Putting yourself first doesn't mean putting others last. You give from overflow, not from depletion.

- Your needs are not inconveniences. They are sacred signals pointing you toward alignment and purpose.

- Nourishing yourself is an act of love for all.

Mantra: *When I honor my needs, I honor my purpose. Nourishing myself is an act of love for all.*

Reconnect

Once you've reclaimed your right to receive, rebuild your life around self-nourishment, not as a luxury but as a daily rhythm.

- Ask yourself what you truly desire, not just what's expected of you. Write it down.

____

____

____

- Create a visual reminder of this desire: a vision board, a sketch, a sticky note. Let it live in your space.

- Identify a few small steps that move you toward this desire. Take one step today.

____

____

____

____

Affirmation: *I deserve to be well, whole, and fully alive. When I care for myself, I rise in service to others from a place of truth and strength.*

Notes:

____

____

____

____

____

____

____

____

____

____

HOLDING GUILT & SHAME TO BECOMING VULNERABLE

"Shame is the intensely painful feeling or experience of believing that we are flawed and therefore unworthy of love and belonging. Shame means, 'I am bad.' Guilt means, 'I did something bad.'"

"When we want greater clarity in our purpose or deeper and more meaningful spiritual lives, vulnerability is the path."

~ Brené Brown

Practices for Releasing Guilt and Shame and Embracing Vulnerability

Guilt and shame are powerful emotions, often rooted in the past but quietly influencing the present. Vulnerability is not weakness. It's the sacred doorway to healing, connection, and freedom.

These practices are meant to help you soften self-judgment, reclaim compassion, and reconnect with your whole self.

Reflect

To release guilt or shame, you must first acknowledge where it lives emotionally, physically, and energetically.

- Recall a specific moment that left you with lingering guilt or shame. What happened, and how did you respond?

____

____

____

- Where did you feel it in your body?

____

____

- Did it show up as tightness, heat, heaviness, or something else?

____

____

____

- Does that moment still carry emotional weight today? If so, what story are you still holding onto?

____

____

____

____

____

____

Journaling Prompt: *What experience still carries guilt or shame in your body?*

____

How has it shaped your self-perception?

____

____

____

____

Are you ready to release that experience?

____

Reframe

Reframing invites compassion to step in and re-tell your story with love and clarity.

- Are you revisiting the past with harsh judgment or with the same grace you would offer someone you love?

____

- Can you offer empathy not only to yourself, but also to others involved in the moment? Everyone was learning.

____

____

____

- What if that moment wasn't a failure, but a necessary part of your becoming?

____

Insight Practice: *What would shift if I viewed this not as a wound to punish, but as a lesson to love myself through?*

Reconnect

Vulnerability is the pathway back to wholeness. True healing happens when you stop hiding your heart from yourself or others.

- What would it look like to be more emotionally honest with yourself, or with someone tied to that pain?

- Express your feelings, not to control their reaction, but to free your own truth. This is *your* release.

- Begin a forgiveness practice like Ho'oponopono, a traditional Hawaiian practice of reconciliation and forgiveness: *"I'm sorry. Please forgive me. Thank you. I love you."* Speak the words slowly. Let the emotion move through you. Try reciting this daily for 40 days. Use rosary or mala beads to guide repetition and deepen healing.

Affirmation: *I release the weight of shame. I forgive myself and others with compassion. I am free to heal, to feel, and to begin again.*

ADDICTION TO AWARENESS

"This is the age of addiction,
a condition so epidemic, so
all-encompassing that you may
not even know if you have it."
~ Russell Brand

How to Cultivate Awareness and Heal Emotional Addiction

Emotional addiction isn't just about substances or behaviors; it's about patterns we cling to in order to feel loved, worthy, or safe. Whether it's the need to be needed, praised, or in control, these patterns often begin as survival mechanisms. Healing them requires self-awareness, gentle reprogramming, and a return to internal stability.

Reflect

Awareness is the first act of healing. By tracing your emotional patterns back to their roots, you begin to reclaim your power.

- Where in your life do you consistently feel unseen, unappreciated, or emotionally depleted?

____

____

____

____

____

- Can you name behaviors that feel compulsive, like over-giving, people-pleasing, or needing constant validation?

____

____

____

____

- What beliefs were modeled for you about what earns love, praise, or a sense of worth?

____

____

____

____

- Who taught you those lessons?

____

Journaling Prompt: *When did you first begin seeking external validation, and from whom?*

____

____

____

Has that shaped how you seek to "prove your value" today?

____

____

____

Reframe

When emotional addiction is a response to early unmet needs, reframing helps to release shame and step into empowered choice.

- Emotional patterns that once protected you may now be limiting your growth, they were tools, not truths.

- Ask yourself honestly: "What am I gaining by repeating this cycle?"

____

____

____

____

- "What am I losing by staying in it?"

____

____

____

____

- Appreciation feels good, but it's not evidence of your worth. You are inherently valuable, even when unseen.

Empowering Question: *What if I gave from fullness instead of fear?*

____

____

____

____

How would it feel to be free from needing a response to feel enough?

____

____

____

Reconnect

Healing emotional addiction means reconnecting to your own internal source of value, and modeling what it means to love yourself first.

- Identify one emotional addiction. Track where and how it appears in your relationships and routines.

- Observe your emotional responses when others don't meet your expectations. Don't judge, just gather insight and compassion for yourself.

- Support your healing with therapy, coaching, or resources like podcasts, books, or trusted communities. You don't have to do it alone.

Affirmation: *I am no longer ruled by the need to be validated. I value myself fully and I give from love, not lack.*

Notes:

____

____

____

____

____

CONDITIONAL TO UNCONDITIONAL LOVE

"Unconditional love is a journey of self-discovery, where we learn to love ourselves fully and extend that love to others."

~ Osho

How to Cultivate Unconditional Self-Love

Unconditional self-love isn't about ignoring flaws. It's about embracing the whole of who you are, even as you grow. It's choosing compassion over critique, presence over performance, and worthiness over waiting. This practice helps you return home to yourself, again and again, with softness, truth, and grace.

Reflect

True self-love begins with honest self-inquiry. You can't fully love yourself until you see the places where love has been withheld.

- Have you done the work to love yourself completely, not just in your strengths, but in your messiness, mistakes, and humanity?

____

____

____

____

- Who in your life do you love unconditionally?

____

____

- What makes it easy (or hard) to do so?

____

____

____

- Are there places where you're still chasing love through perfection, approval, or productivity?

____

____

____

____

Journaling Prompt: *Where in my life is my self-love still conditional?*

____

____

____

What would it look like to love myself without needing to be "better" first?

____

____

____

Reframe

Self-love is a daily practice you choose. When you stop outsourcing love, you start reclaiming your power.

- Unconditional love must begin with the self. No one else can give you what you're unwilling to offer yourself.

- Conditional self-love often hides in phrases like "I'll love myself when…" Or, "Once I achieve this, then I'll rest." What if right now is enough?

- Loving yourself in the "messy middle" is radical. It's a declaration: I am worthy here, too.

Empowering Question: *What would shift if I chose to love myself, not later, but now, as I am?*

———————————————————————

———————————————————————

———————————————————————

———————————————————————

Reconnect

Unconditional self-love becomes real through how you speak to yourself, care for yourself, and honor your needs daily.

- Make a list of small ways to show yourself love today: saying no without apology, speaking gently to yourself, resting without guilt.

———————————————————————

———————————————————————

———————————————————————

———————————————————————

- Set boundaries with those who deplete you, even if you care about them. Your energy matters.

- Practice receiving love from others without deflection or downplaying. Let love land. Let it nourish you.

Affirmation: *I am worthy of love without conditions. I choose to love, protect, and honor myself fully, freely, and now.*

Notes:

____

____

____

____

____

____

____

____

____

____

____

____

PROJECTING TO PROTECTING

"Don't take anything personally. Nothing others do is because of you. What others say and do is a projection of their own reality, their own dream. When you are immune to the opinions and actions of others, you won't be the victim of needless suffering."
~ Don Miguel Ruiz

How to Support Without Projecting

True support is not about fixing, rescuing, or redirecting. It's about creating space for someone to access their own wisdom, in their own time. When we release the need to project our past onto someone else's present, we offer the powerful gift of presence, not prescription.

Reflect

Before offering guidance, pause to examine your motivation. Self-awareness helps you give support from a place of clarity rather than assumption.

- Reflect on a time you gave advice based more on *your* experience than the other person's reality. What was driving you?

- Have you ever regretted offering guidance that didn't land or wasn't truly aligned with their needs?

____

____

____

____

- Consider moments when your urge to protect may have disrupted someone else's opportunity to grow, stumble, or decide for themselves.

Journaling Prompt: *When have I offered support from a place of fear, memory, or control?*

____

____

____

____

How might I shift toward curiosity and trust instead?

____

____

____

____

Reframe

Let go of the belief that love must look like intervention. Empowerment often looks like stepping back.

- Supporting someone doesn't mean directing their path; it means believing in their ability to find it.

- Your lived experience is valuable, but it's not the universal truth. Their story may unfold differently and beautifully.

- Asking thoughtful, reflective questions creates space for insight. It's often more helpful than offering pre-packaged advice.

Empowering Question: *What if the most loving thing I can offer is not my answer but my trust in their own?*

Reconnect

Choose presence over projection. Hold space for someone else's process with humility, warmth, and restraint.

- When someone seeks your guidance, pause. Listen first. Then ask questions that draw out their own clarity: "What do you feel drawn to?" "What are you afraid of?"

- "What choice brings peace to your body, not just your mind?"

- Be aware of your tone and energy. Curiosity fosters openness. Certainty can raise defenses.

- If you recognize what you've projected, acknowledge it with grace. Reconnect through honesty: "I realize I made this about me. Thank you for your patience."

Affirmation: *I support with presence, not pressure. I trust your journey. I honor your timing. I let love listen.*

Notes:

DECISION MAKING FROM THE SUBCONSCIOUS TO FREE WILL

*"I am an artist, and I have
the ability and the free will to
choose how the world
will envision me."*

~ *Lady Gaga*

How to Reclaim Free Will and Make Conscious Decisions

True freedom begins when you stop living by default and start living by design. Reclaiming your free will means identifying where you've been on autopilot, interrupting fear-based programming, and stepping boldly into self-authored choices. Your life is a sacred creation. You are the one holding the tools.

Reflect

Before you can choose consciously, you must first become aware of where you've been choosing unconsciously.

- Reflect on major life decisions, relationships, careers, lifestyle, that felt more reactive than rooted in your own values.

- Consider moments where you avoided or delayed a decision to maintain someone else's comfort rather than honor your truth.

- Identify where fear, self-doubt, or limiting beliefs may still be steering your actions (e.g., "Don't rock the boat," "Stay small," "Play it safe").

Journaling Prompt: *When have you given away your power by avoiding truth, deferring to others, or operating from fear?*

What would reclaiming that power look like now?

Reframe

You're not just a passenger in your life, you're the driver. Reframing helps you take the wheel with clarity, purpose, and self-trust.

- You are the author of your life. Reclaim the pen. Rewrite the script.

- Start with your vision: On your last day, what do you want to have created, contributed, and become? Let that legacy inform today's choices.

- Mistakes are not failures, they're feedback. Every wrong turn helps sharpen your inner compass.

Empowering Question: *If you lived from your desires instead of your fears, what decisions would you make today?*

____

____

____

____

Reconnect

Free will requires consistent alignment. Anchor into your vision daily and make choices that honor the life you're here to build.

- Make a sacred contract with yourself: no more settling. Write your vision down. Speak it aloud. Let it shape your filters: What stays?

____

____

- What is going?

____

____

- Who expands me?

____

____

- Who drains me?

____

____

- Choose your inputs with discernment. Reduce exposure to the noise of polarizing news and negative media. Nourish your spirit with truth, beauty, and possibility.

- Establish grounding practices of meditation, prayer, breathwork, or visualization. Let each morning become a return to your values, your vision, your voice.

Affirmation: *I am a conscious creator. I choose from love, not fear. Each decision is a step toward the life I am meant to live.*

Notes:

____

____

____

____

____

____

____

____

____

____

____

AVOIDANCE TO ENGAGEMENT

"Engage your life with enthusiasm, grasp your life aggressively and squeeze from it every drop of excitement, satisfaction and joy."
~ Felix Baumgartner

How to Move from Avoidance to Engagement

Avoidance is often a shield, one that forms in response to fear, rejection, or overwhelm. But connection is a deep human need, and true engagement doesn't require perfection, only presence. When we meet others with curiosity and courage, we begin to dissolve the distance we've built.

Reflect

To engage authentically, you must first understand what's holding you back.

- Where are you currently avoiding connection?

____

____

____

____

____

____

- Is it in relationships, community, or even with yourself?

____

____

____

- What lies beneath that hesitation?

____

____

____

- Have past experiences of judgment, rejection, or misunderstanding made you reluctant to reach out?

____

____

____

- Is fear keeping you from being fully seen, heard, or known?

____

____

____

____

- Are there people you're drawn to but haven't approached?

____

____

____

____

- If you assumed people wanted to connect with you, could you act from that truth instead of fear?

____

____

____

____

Journaling Prompt: *What fears or past experiences are fueling my avoidance?*

____

____

____

____

Where am I longing for connection but holding back and why?

____

____

____

____

Reframe

Avoidance feels like protection, but it often leads to deeper loneliness. When you reframe connection as a courageous act, you take the first step toward healing.

- Avoidance may feel safe, but it also reinforces the belief that you're not welcome or wanted. That belief is rarely true.

- Most people are waiting for someone to go first. A small gesture can open the door to a meaningful bond.

- You don't need perfect words or timing. Curiosity is enough. Kindness is enough. You are enough!

Empowering Question: *What if I assumed people wanted to connect with me and acted from that truth instead of fear?*

____

____

____

____

Reconnect

Engagement doesn't require intensity. It begins with presence, consistency, and a willingness to show up imperfectly but authentically.

- Challenge yourself to initiate one genuine connection each day, even if it's as simple as a compliment or a question.

- Revisit someone you've recently met. Reach out. Follow up. Ask about something they shared.

- Spark small conversations using easy prompts:
  - "What's a book or podcast that's inspired you lately?"
  - "What's something small that made you smile today?"
  - "What's one thing you're curious about right now?"

Affirmation: *I am open to connection. I release fear and step into curiosity, knowing that presence is enough.*

Notes:

____

____

____

____

____

____

____

____

____

____

____

Notes:

KNOW THY SELF TO KNOWING THY SELF

*"Knowing others is intelligence;
knowing yourself is true wisdom."*
                              ~ Lao Tzu

*"There are three extremely
hard things: steel, a
diamond, and to know oneself."*
                    ~ Benjamin Franklin

How to Know Ourselves

Self-awareness is about liberation, not judgment. When we take an honest look at our patterns, wounds, and protection strategies, we reclaim our power. The goal is to be fully seen, and by ourselves first.

Reflect

Start by looking at the patterns that keep showing up, not with shame but with curiosity.

- What's your personal pitfall?

____

____

____

____

____

____

____

- What's the behavior or belief that repeats itself in your most important relationships?

____

____

____

____

- Where do you feel stuck, misunderstood, or like you're not fully seen?

____

____

____

____

- Is this a familiar feeling from earlier in life?

____

____

____

____

- Are you giving away your power to avoid conflict? Or trying to control others as a way to feel safe?

____

____

____

____

- Can you remember a time you silenced your truth to keep the peace?

____

____

____

____

Journaling Prompt: *What pattern do you see repeating in your relationships or decisions?*

____

____

____

____

What part of you believes this is necessary for love, safety, or belonging?

____

____

____

____

Reframe

Awareness is not punishment; it's a return to truth. You don't need to fix yourself to be worthy. You just need to *know* yourself.

- Knowing your patterns doesn't mean you're broken; it means you're awake.

- Self-awareness is not self-blame. It's the doorway to freedom and intentional living.

- You don't need to over-give or self-sacrifice to earn love. Your boundaries are valid. Your needs are sacred.

Mantra: *Knowing my patterns sets me free. I don't have to be perfect to be powerful.*

Reconnect

Knowing yourself is the beginning. Reconnecting to your truth and living with it is the transformation.

- Reflect on recurring relational dynamics. Identify your part with honesty, but also with self-compassion.

- Write a personal contract for how you want to show up moving forward: "I will honor my voice." "I will choose an aligned connection over approval." "I will not betray myself in order to belong."

- Ask for honest feedback from someone you trust: "What's it like to be in a relationship with me?" Use their perspective as a tool, not a verdict.

Affirmation: *I can know my shadow and still be worthy of love, growth, and connection. I am evolving, sacred, and real.*

Notes:

____

____

____

____

____

____

KARMA TO DHARMA

"If you want to transform your karma to a more desirable experience, look for the seed of opportunity within every adversity, and tie that seed of opportunity to your dharma, or purpose in life. This will enable you to convert the adversity into a benefit and transform the karma into a totally new expression."

~ Deepak Chopra

How to Turn Karma (Heal Self) into Dharma (Heal Others)

Your deepest wounds often hold the seeds of your greatest purpose. Karma teaches you. Dharma serves others. When you heal what once hurt you, you gain wisdom and also the power to walk with others through their own dark nights. You don't need to be perfect to be purposeful. You just need to be willing.

Reflect

Transformation begins with reflection. What once broke you might now be your most sacred offering.

- What is the greatest challenge or karmic wound you've moved through in your life?

____

____

____

____

- What truths did it reveal, not just about your situation, but about your inner strength, patterns, or potential?

____

____

____

____

- Did anyone support or guide you through it?

____

____

____

____

- Was there a person, practice, or resource that lit the way?

____

____

____

____

Journaling Prompt: *What part of my story once felt heavy, but now holds wisdom?*

____

____

____

____

How might it serve someone who's where I once was?

____

____

____

____

Reframe

Your karma is not your shame, it's your foundation. Dharma isn't about being a savior. It's about being a mirror, a companion, a light.

- Karmic lessons aren't punishments, they are sacred invitations to evolve, awaken, and embody compassion.

- Dharma doesn't require a platform or profession. It shows up in everyday moments: listening, guiding, sharing, holding space.

- You don't need credentials to be of service. You need authenticity. Your story alone can be medicine.

Mantra: *My wounds have become wisdom. My story is sacred. I serve from love, not perfection.*

Reconnect

Now that you've walked through fire, offer your light. Dharma is simply love in action.

- Give back to the spaces that once held you: volunteer, donate, or support someone walking a similar path.

- Turn your healing into a roadmap. Write down what helped you: the tools, turning points, and truths. Share it with a friend, a blog, or a circle.

- Reach out. Be the one to say, "I've been there too. I don't have all the answers, but I'm here." That offering alone can change a life.

Affirmation: *I transform my healing into service. My past has purpose. I am here to love, guide, and walk with others in truth.*

Notes:

IMPATIENCE TO PATIENT

*"To lose patience is
to lose the battle."*
~ Mahatma Gandhi

Trusting the Timing You Cannot Yet See

Cultivating patience isn't about becoming passive. It's about becoming present. This chapter invites you to turn patience into revelation, allowing your waiting seasons to deepen your faith, not drain your hope.

Reflect

Lack of patience often masks the deeper wisdom. Reflection asks you to slow down and examine what's happening underneath your urgency. Impatience is about what you fear. What is that fear? Naming the root of your agitation allows space for transformation.

- **Identify the Source**
  Where are you clinging, pushing, or rushing for an answer, resolution, or outcome?

____

____

____

____

____

____

- **Name the Root**
  What is truly beneath your impatience? Is it fear, grief, desire, uncertainty, excitement? Naming it brings clarity and softness.

____

____

____

____

- **Understand the Lesson**
  What is my impatience here to teach me?

____

____

____

____

- What is it asking me to notice or to surrender?

____

____

____

____

Journaling Prompt: *What's really beneath this impatience and what would it feel like to trust instead of push?*

____

____

____

Reframe

Patience is not resignation. It's choosing grace over grasping. It's choosing to believe that things are working out even when they are not visible. Every moment of waiting can become a moment of awakening.

- **Shift the Perspective**
  Patience isn't weakness. It's wisdom cloaked in grace. It takes far more strength to trust than to control.

- **Transform the Energy**
  Turn impatience into trust. Let frustration become a prayer. Gratitude is the bridge that carries you from agitation to peace.

- **Discern What's Yours to Carry**
  Ask Yourself: "Do I have control here?"
  – If yes, take aligned, present action.
  – If not, surrender. The universe is already working behind the scenes.

Mantra: *"Patience Pays. Wait. Let the hand of God work for you. Lean on Him, and all good things will come to you. The One who has made you will take care of you." ~ Yogi Bhajan*

Reconnect

Reconnection is about coming home to the real world, not the fantasy of control or the fear of delay. Your breath is enough. The moment is enough. There is beauty in being where you are, even when you don't yet know where it's leading.

- **Anchor in the Present**
  Sit in stillness. Breathe deeply. Place your hand over your heart. Feel what's true right now and release what's not yours to solve today.

- **Trust the Timing**
  Life is unfolding on time, even if it's not on your moment now. Everything, even now, is working for your good.

- **Create a Grounding Ritual**
  – Light a candle.
  – Take a walk without your phone.
  – Repeat your chosen mantra while placing one hand on your belly, one on your heart.

Affirmation: *I release the need to rush. I trust the unfolding. What is meant for me is already finding its way.*

Notes:

____

____

____

____

____

____

____

____

____

____

____

TURBULENCE TO STILLNESS

"The quieter you become,
the more you can hear."

~ Ram Dass

Stillness Is Your Superpower

Turbulence is part of life but it doesn't have to define your inner world. Stillness isn't about escaping the storm. It's about learning how to return to your center within it. This chapter invites you to meet overwhelm with presence, shift your state through breath, and find clarity where there was chaos.

Reflect

Reflection is the first step to understanding your stress responses and softening them. Turbulent times can feel like they control us, but often, what's needed is awareness. When you pause to look back with compassion, you begin to see where your true power lies.

- Recall a recent moment of overwhelm or stress.

- What triggered it? An event, a conversation, a thought spiral?

____

____

____

____

____

- How did your body respond: shallow breath, quickened pulse, racing thoughts?

____

____

____

____

- How long did it take to return to calm? Or have you still not completely returned?

____

____

____

Journaling Prompt: *What was my body trying to tell me in that moment of stress and how can I honor it differently next time?*

____

____

____

____

Reframe

Reframing helps you remember that your breath is not just a bodily function. It's an emotional and spiritual tool. Stillness doesn't require silence around you. It asks for intention within you. You don't have to wait for peace to come from outside. You can create it inside yourself, breath by breath.

- Your breath is a direct line to your nervous system. It offers you a choice: reactivity or rest.

- You don't have to control everything. You only need to regulate *yourself.*

- Stillness is not the absence of difficulty. It's the presence of awareness.

Mantra: *With every breath, I return to balance.*

Practice: Alternate Nostril Breathing (Nadi Shodhana)

This ancient technique balances the left and right hemispheres of the brain and gently calms the nervous system.

1. Sit comfortably. Close your eyes.

2. Use your right thumb to close your right nostril. Inhale slowly through the left.

3. Close the left nostril with your ring finger. Release the thumb. Exhale slowly through the right.

4. Inhale through the right nostril. Close it. Exhale through the left.

5. Continue for 2–5 minutes. Let your breath guide you back to your center.

Mantra: *With every breath, I return to balance.*

Reconnect

Reconnection allows you to revisit a difficult moment, but with stillness rather than stress. The situation may remain but your relationship to it will change. Stillness helps you respond instead of react. It helps you see what's truly yours to carry and what can be released.

- **Revisit the Situation in Your Mind**
  Has your emotional state shifted? Can you see it with more clarity now?

____

____

____

____

- **Ask Yourself**
  "What wisdom is available to me now that wasn't before?" "What does my calm self know that my stressed self forgot?"

____

____

____

____

- **An Anchor in the Storm**
  Stillness doesn't eliminate the storm. It anchors you through it. You don't need the world to be quiet to feel peace. You only need to return to yourself. Trust that you can be still, even during chaos.

Affirmation: *In every breath, I find my calm. I return to my center. I trust that I can be still, even here.*

Notes:

____

____

____

____

HEAVEN TO EARTH

"Heaven on Earth is a
choice you must make,
not a place you must find."
~ *Dr. Wayne Dyer*

Choosing Heaven Now

We are taught to believe heaven is somewhere far away, a reward "for later." But heaven is not distant. It's available in every sacred breath, every moment of presence, every act of love. This chapter invites you to stop waiting and start witnessing. What you long for is not "for later." It's for now.

Reflect

Reflection is the doorway to presence. Begin by noticing how you've postponed your joy. You've tied it to a milestone, a future version of yourself, or an external success.

- What joy, truth, or beauty have you been postponing, waiting for "someday"?

____

____

____

____

____

____

- Are you withholding your full presence now, believing fulfillment comes after a goal is reached?

____

____

____

____

- What might shift if you stopped delaying delight and chose to experience the light right now?

____

____

____

____

Journaling Prompt: *Where in your life are you waiting for permission to enjoy what is already here?*

____

____

____

____

Reframe

Reframing allows you to see that heaven is a decision rather than a destination. It's a lens, a way of being. The divine is not out of reach. It lives in every ordinary moment, if you are willing to pause and see it. Nothing needs to change except the way you look at it.

- Heaven isn't a future reward , it's a perspective shift.

- Ask Yourself: "What already feels sacred, beautiful,

or divine?"
– The warmth of a hug.
– The quiet after rain.
– A shared laugh.
– A kind word.
– A deep breath.

- Let the present moment be enough.
  Heaven doesn't wait.
  It welcomes.

Mantra: *I open my eyes to heaven here and now. Beauty is already around me. Peace is already possible.*

Reconnect

Reconnection is the practice of remembering that the sacred is available in every moment, not just in ritual but in rhythm. Heaven isn't somewhere you arrive. It's something you cultivate. When you slow down and bless what is, you create a life that feels like home to your soul.

- **Create a Ritual of Presence**
  – Say a daily gratitude prayer, simple, heartfelt, true.
  – Walk barefoot in nature. Let the earth remind you that you belong.
  – Light a candle and bless your space with love.
  – Hug like it's holy, with intention and with atten-

tion. Let each moment matter (because it does).

- **Be Present in the Now**
  Stop waiting to arrive. You're already here. Let your ordinary life become an extraordinary offering.

Affirmation: *I will experience today, as if I were living in heaven.*

Notes:

____

____

____

____

____

____

____

____

____

____

____

____

POSSESSIONS TO GIFTS

*"There is nothing about
a caterpillar that tells you
it's going to be a butterfly."*
~ R. Buckminster Fuller

Letting Go to Let Life In

Holding on too tightly can close the very doors you're meant to walk through. Sometimes what you think you're protecting is actually what's preventing your peace. This chapter invites you to soften your grip on outcomes, identities, and attachments. Trust that when you let go, you don't lose control. You gain alignment.

Reflect

Reflection helps you identify the places in your life where grasping has replaced grace. Are you clinging from fear, from habit, or from some meaning assigned long ago? Often it's not the thing itself that keeps us stuck. It's what we've decided it means. Awareness creates room for surrender.

- What are you holding too tightly? Is it an identity, a relationship, a possession, a belief?

____

____

____

____

____

- Ask Yourself: "What am I afraid will happen if I let go?"

____

____

____

____

- Are you attached to the thing itself or to what it symbolizes?

____

____

____

____

Journaling Prompt: *What's something I once lost that made space for something better?*

____

____

____

____

What did I learn from that shift?

____

____

____

____

Reframe

Reframing lets you shift from ownership to appreciation. Everything in your life is a gift, not a guarantee. Releasing doesn't mean erasing. It means honoring what was and making space for what's next. You can love fully without holding tightly.

- Shift from "This is mine" to "This was a gift I got to experience."

- Let gratitude replace grasping.

- Honor what someone or something brought into your life even if their chapter is complete.

Mantra: *I release what no longer serves me and trust something greater is on its way.*

Reconnect

Reconnection is about replacing attachment with presence. When you love with openness, not ownership, you create space for true connection, with others, with life, and with yourself. Freedom is not the absence of care. It is the absence of control.

- **Ask Yourself**
  "Am I loving this person or clinging to who I want them to be?" "Am I gripping this path or walking it with trust?"

____

____

____

- **Honor Diverging Paths**
  Let go with blessing. Trust that honoring another's journey does not diminish your own.

- **Practice a Ritual of Release**
  Write a short letter of gratitude and release to someone or something you're ready to hold more lightly. Let it be your offering of freedom, for them and for you.

Affirmation: *I open my hands. I open my heart. I trust that letting go makes space for what is true.*

Notes:

____

____

____

____

____

____

____

____

____

____

____

____

____

RESIST TO SURRENDER

"Surrender happens spontaneously with the knowledge that you are not in control of anything, not even your thoughts or feelings. When you realize that you are not in control of your life, but some supreme law governs life, then surrender happens."
~ *Gurudev Sri Sri Ravi Shankar*

The Strength of Surrendering to the Unseen

Resistance is often a response to fear of losing control, of being disappointed, of being asked to wait. But what if the unknown isn't a threat, it's a threshold? This chapter invites you to soften your grip on outcomes, trust what you cannot yet see, and allow grace to carry what your mind can't hold. Surrender is not a failure of effort, it's the highest form of wisdom.

Reflect

Reflection allows you to notice where tension is still alive in your thoughts, your body, your heart. Resistance often shows up as control, urgency, or a clenched desire to make something happen.

Try naming what you're trying to force, and why:

- Where in your life are you still resisting a truth, a change, a call to trust?

____

____

____

____

- What outcome, desire, or situation are you gripping tightly?

____

____

____

____

- Ask Yourself: "Why am I trying to control what I have no control over?"

____

____

____

____

Journaling Prompt: *What am I resisting right now, and what is that costing me, emotionally, spiritually, or energetically?*

____

____

____

____

Reframe

Reframing invites you to replace the myth of control with the medicine of trust. Surrender is not failure. You are stepping into partnership with something wiser and more loving than your fear. Resistance contracts. Surrender expands. The outcome may still be unknown, but your posture can shift from tightness to trust.

- Let go of this belief: "If I don't control it, I'll lose it." Replace it with: "If I trust, what's meant for me will stay and what's not will gently fall away."

- Surrender isn't weakness. It's strength in partnership with divine timing and guidance.

- You're not giving up. You're giving over to love, to grace, and to your soul's deeper rhythm.

Mantra: *I release control. I allow love, guidance, and grace to lead.*

Reconnect

Reconnection is about returning to the wisdom that already lives within you. That wisdom is not the voice of fear, but the whisper of intuition. When you release the need to know everything, you make space for true knowing to emerge. The answers may not come instantly, but the peace will.

- **When Fear or Urgency Rises, Return to Presence**
  Let your body become the altar. Let stillness become the prayer. Here's a simple five-step practice:
  1. Sit quietly with eyes closed.
  2. Rest both palms open on your lap as a gesture of trust.
  3. Breathe deeply and slowly.
  4. Whisper: "Why have you placed this desire inside my heart?" "What would you have me do next?"
  5. Listen. Wait. The response may come in a word, a symbol, a breath, or a quiet sense of peace.

Affirmation: *I trust what I cannot yet see. I surrender to what is true, aligned, and guided by love.*

Notes:

Part Two

QUEENSHIP

AWAKEN YOUR ROYAL SELF THROUGH EMPOWERED & AUTHENTIC LIVING

WOMAN TO WOMEN

Women Rising Together

Comparison is a thief of joy and connection. When we compare, we isolate. When we celebrate, we build something sacred. This chapter invites you to shift from quiet competition to collaboration. When one woman rises, it's not a threat, it's a mirror. The same light lives in you.

Reflect

Reflection invites you to take an honest look at how subtle comparison may be impacting your relationships with other women. The voice of competition is often quiet, but cloaked in insecurity and judgment:

- Are you subtly competing with, rather than celebrating, other women?

____

____

____

____

____

- When another woman shines, do you feel inspired, or slightly diminished?

____

____

____

____

- Where might quiet comparison, self-doubt, or withheld celebration be blocking your capacity for real sisterhood?

____

____

____

____

Journaling Prompt: *Where in my life am I withholding celebration or support for another woman and what's the story behind it?*

____

____

____

____

____

____

____

Reframe

Reframing allows you to see that sisterhood is not a scarcity game. It's a sacred circle. Another woman's power doesn't diminish yours. It affirms what's possible. True empowerment multiplies when it's shared freely, without performance or pretense.

- Sisterhood is not a threat, it's sacred.

- Imagine what becomes possible when we choose connection over quiet rivalry.

- There is enough space, enough success, and enough light for all of us to rise.

Mantra: *When one woman rises, we all rise.*

Reconnect

Reconnection is the daily practice of choosing collaboration over comparison. But the village you long for may not arrive on its own. It must be built with intention, vulnerability, and love. Start small. Start now.

- **Build the Village Intentionally**
  Choose three women this week to support with presence and sincerity:
  – Send a thoughtful message of affirmation or encouragement
  – Share a resource, opportunity, or uplifting story
  – Invite them into a moment of joy, reflection, or ritual

- **Take the Action**
  Don't wait for a crisis to show up for one another. Let support become your lifestyle. Not just a gesture, but a rhythm.

Affirmation: *I choose connection over comparison. I rise with others, not in spite of them. Sisterhood is my strength.*

Notes:

____

____

____

____

____

____

____

____

____

____

____

____

____

SERVANT TO QUEEN

"The strength of a realm comes from its King; the strength of the King comes from his Queen."
~ Cody Edward Lee Miller

Claiming the Crown Over Self-Sacrifice

There is a version of service that uplifts and there is a version that depletes. Many women are conditioned to give endlessly, to wear sacrifice as a badge of honor. But true Sovereignty is found in balance, not burnout.

This chapter invites you to rise from duty into dignity, to stop abandoning yourself in the name of care, and to wear your Crown with clarity, grace, and unapologetic worth.

Reflect

Reflection helps you explore the roles you've taken on, consciously or unconsciously, in your relationships. Caregiving, nurturing, and leading are powerful expressions of love. But when they come at the cost of your own well-being, they become cages instead of Crowns.

- How do you see yourself in your closest relationships? Caregiver, fixer, nurturer, leader, Queen?

____

____

____

____

- Where in your life do you feel like you're constantly serving without being replenished in return?

____

____

____

____

- What beliefs, upbringing, or cultural messages taught you that others' needs come before you own?

____

____

____

____

Journaling Prompt: *Where in my life am I still operating from duty, rather than from worth?*

____

____

____

____

____

____

____

____

Reframe

Honoring yourself is not selfish, it's Sovereign. The Queen archetype is about reigning with self-respect, sacred boundaries, and emotional maturity. You are allowed to receive. You are allowed to rest. You are allowed to rise.

- Serving with love is noble, but not at the cost of self-abandonment.

- Being a Queen means honoring your own needs with the same devotion you offer others.

- You can nurture and receive. You can support and be supported. This is not a contradiction; it is wholeness.

Empowering Question: *What small but powerful shifts can I make today to step more fully into my queenship?*

____

____

____

____

____

____

____

Reconnect

Reconnection is about occupying your full worth and inviting others to meet you there. When you lead from wholeness you don't need to be everything for everyone. You show others what it means to live with grace, strength, and self-respect.

- **Invite Your Circle In**
  Let others witness the woman you are becoming. Don't dim your light for comfort. Share your truth, with love and clarity.

- **Model Sovereign Self-Leadership**
  Communicate your needs. Celebrate your milestones. Receive compliments, care, and praise without apology.

- **Celebrate Yourself**
  Not as a reward, but as a rhythm. Let your life reflect your worth before anyone else does.

Affirmation: *I am a Queen. I honor my worth, I receive with grace, and I inspire others to rise with me.*

Notes:

____

____

____

____

____

____

____

____

____

____

JEALOUSY TO ADMIRATION

"Never hate jealous people.
They are jealous because
they think you're
better than them."

~ Paulo Coelho

Shifting from Comparison to Expansion

Jealousy is not a flaw, it's a flag. It's a signal that something within you is being stirred, awakened, or waiting to be expressed. When you meet that feeling with curiosity instead of shame, you gain access to your own untapped potential. This chapter invites you to alchemize envy into admiration and turn comparison into motivation.

Reflect

Reflection allows you to look beneath the surface of jealousy. The emotion itself is not wrong. It often reveals a deep longing, a waking dream, or a quality you're ready to claim for yourself. Begin with real honesty:

- Who have you felt jealous of recently?

- What specifically triggered that feeling?

____

____

____

____

- Was it their relationship, success, confidence, ease, or lifestyle?

____

____

____

____

- What quality in them are you truly admiring and what does it awaken in you?

____

____

____

____

Journaling Prompt: *What desire or potential in me is being stirred by this feeling?*

____

____

____

____

____

What is it asking me to notice or nurture?

Reframe

Reframing allows you to shift jealousy from self-judgment into soul guidance. What you admire in someone else is not proof that you've failed. It's proof that something similar may be possible for you. Let their light become your map, not your shadow.

- Jealousy is not always a sign of lack. It can be a signal of longing, a desire waiting for permission.

- Instead of seeing their success as a threat, see it as proof that it can be done.

- Ask yourself: "What habits, choices, or mindset might I learn from their journey?"

Insight Practice: *Recall a time you turned comparison into motivation. What did you do differently and what was the outcome?*

How did your energy shift when you focused on your own path with clarity and courage?

Reconnect

Reconnection is the moment when you consciously choose to celebrate others as a way to expand yourself. The energy you pour into admiration rather than comparison uplifts everyone, including yourself. Sisterhood, expansion, and Sovereignty are built there.

- **Choose Admiration Consciously**
  Let others' greatness be a mirror, not a measuring stick. Use their light to reveal your own.

- **Celebrate Over Compete**
  Text someone your appreciation. Compliment a peer's work. Speak admiration out loud. Watch how your own energy expands.

- **Anchor the Shift**
  The more you celebrate what you see in others, the more you awaken what's waiting in you.

Affirmation: *I admire the greatness in others as a reflection of what is rising within me. There is no lack only limitless possibility.*

Notes:

DAMSEL IN DISTRESS TO WONDER WOMAN

"She was powerful not
because she wasn't scared,
but because she went on so
strongly, despite the fear."

~ Atticus

Step Into Your Power and Practice Self-Leadership

Self-leadership begins when you stop waiting and start trusting. It's not about controlling every outcome, it's about showing up in full ownership of your choices, your voice, and your truth. In every moment you reclaim your power from doubt, distraction, or dependency, you step deeper into your Sovereignty. This chapter invites you to move from reaction to responsibility, from seeking validation to standing in quiet, embodied wisdom.

Reflect

Reflection allows you to witness the habits and stories that shape how you respond to challenge and choice. Often, we give our power away by waiting, deferring, or shrinking.

Self-leadership begins when you stop waiting and start trusting. It means showing up in full ownership of your choices, your voice, and your truth. It's reclaiming your power from doubt, distraction, or dependency.

- In times of stress or uncertainty, do you lead or retreat?

____

____

____

____

- What does your response say about how much you trust yourself?

____

____

____

____

- Are you waiting for someone else to save you; a partner, boss, mentor or friend?

____

____

____

____

Journaling Prompt: *Where in my life am I outsourcing power that is mine to claim?*

____

____

____

____

Reframe

Reframing helps you move from fear to freedom. You don't need to discover your power, you only need to remember it. You know how to listen and respond with integrity. Moments of uncertainty are invitations to lead, not from ego but from essence.

- Reclaim your power not with pressure, but with grounded self-worth.

- Ask yourself: "Am I seeking advice to gain clarity or because I fear making the wrong choice?"

____

____

____

____

- True strength isn't loud. It's the quiet confidence of trusting your own wisdom.

Empowering Question: *What would shift if I moved from seeking approval to trusting my inner voice?*

____

____

____

____

Reconnect

Reconnection means returning to the wisdom within you and acting from it daily. Self-leadership is about presence. You embody your power and you lead by example.

- **Find Inspiration**
  - Think of a woman you admire for her strength.
  - What qualities does she embody?

____

____

____

____

  - Where and how can you begin to practice those qualities?

____

____

____

____

- **Name Your Superpower**
  - What's the unique way you naturally lead, love, create, or guide?

____

____

  - Is it your clarity? Your warmth? Your vision? Your steadiness?

____

____

  - Let that superpower guide how you speak, decide, and show up every day.

Affirmation: *I trust my intuition. I lead with strength and softness. I am not waiting to be saved. I already have everything I need to rise.*

GIVING TO RECEIVING

*"Most women are starving
to receive something that they
need to give to themselves."*
~ Sherry Argov

The Power of Receiving

Giving may come naturally. Receiving can feel unfamiliar, even uncomfortable. Yet true connection requires both. Receiving isn't a weakness. It ought to be an act of trust. It says, "I am open. I am worthy. I am willing to be nourished." This chapter invites you to soften the walls around your heart to let love, care, and support move freely from you and to you.

Reflect

Reflection helps you examine the deeply rooted beliefs you may attach to receiving. For many this stirs guilt, discomfort, and a sense of indebtedness.

- What is your current relationship with receiving?

____

____

____

____

- Do you feel guilt, awkwardness, or comfort when someone offers love, help, or kindness?

____

____

- Think of a recent moment when someone gave you a compliment, a gift, or words of support.
  - How did you respond?
  - What emotions came up?

____

____

____

____

Journaling Prompt: *What do my reactions to receiving reveal about my beliefs around worthiness or independence?*

____

____

____

____

____

____

Reframe

Reframing allows you to see receiving not as passivity, but as sacred participation. In many spiritual traditions, especially feminine ones , receptivity is not optional. It is essential. You were never meant to pour out endlessly without being filled.

- Receiving is not a weakness. It's a vital part of connection and feminine energy.

- Let go of the belief that you must earn support or prove your value to be cared for.

- How do you want to feel when you receive?
  – Safe?
  – Seen?
  – Soft?
  – Grateful?

____

____

____

____

Those feelings are not rewards. They are your feminine birthrights.

Empowering Thought: *Receiving is not taking; it's allowing love to flow both ways.*

Reconnect

Reconnection is allowing love to flow both ways. Receiving with grace affirms your worth and mirrors that worth to others. You teach the world how to love you well.

- **Practice Receptive Energy Intentionally**
  Ask: "What is one small thing I can receive today without guilt or apology?"
  - A kind word
  - A helping hand
  - A compliment
  - Rest
  - Pleasure
  - Praise

____

____

- **Let "Thank You" Be Enough**
  Resist the urge to deflect, minimize, or repay. Simply receive. Let the gift land.

- **Tune Into the Shift**
  Notice how your body and spirit respond when you allow yourself to be nourished.

Affirmation: *I receive with open arms, an open heart, and deep gratitude. I am worthy of love, care, and support just as I am.*

Notes:

INDECISIVE TO INTERNAL KNOWING

"Be established within yourself."
~ *Yogi Bhajan*

Coming Home to Your Own Voice

In a world of noise, advice, and endless opinions, it's easy to lose touch with your own truth. Sovereignty begins when you start honoring the guidance that's already within you. This chapter invites you to quiet the outside world, reconnect to your inner compass, and remember that clear answers rise from your own stillness and not from consensus.

Reflect

Reflection invites you to witness where you've been deferring your power. If external seeking replaces inner trust, it creates disconnection from who you really are.

Notice how you've been giving your voice away, and why:

- When do you most often seek advice from others?

____

____

____

____

____

____

- What emotions are you avoiding by outsourcing decisions?

____

____

____

____

- What current decision in your life needs your own voice, not someone else's permission or opinion?

____

____

____

____

Journaling Prompt: *What am I truly seeking when I ask for advice and what part of me already knows the answer?*

____

____

____

____

Reframe

Advice can be helpful, but only if it serves your truth. You are here to live by conviction, not by committee.

- External input can offer perspective, but inner Sovereignty begins with self-trust.

- Reconnect with your core values. They are your soul's compass.

- Look back: What past decisions left you feeling proud, peaceful, or powerful?

____

____

____

____

  – What guided you then?

____

____

____

  – What can you reclaim from those moments now?

____

____

____

____

Empowering Thought: *Your clearest answers rise from within, not from consensus.*

Reconnect

Reconnection means hearing your own voice again. When you get quiet, what's true for you begins to surface. Sovereignty doesn't require loudness. It requires presence. Begin small, but begin within.

- **Create Intentional Space for Clarity**
  – Journal without filters.
  – Meditate with a single question in your heart.

– Take long walks without your phone or distractions.
– Let quiet become your guide.
– Let your body respond before your mind intervenes.
– Notice the wisdom that arises
– Trust that the answers are already within you.

Affirmation: *I trust my inner wisdom. I make decisions from a place of clarity, love, and alignment. My truth lives within me.*

Notes:

____

____

____

____

____

____

____

____

____

____

____

____

____

PERCEPTION TO REALITY

"Perception is reality."

~ Lee Atwater

Becoming the Woman You Already Are

Your self-perception is the foundation of your Sovereignty. It informs how you speak, move, lead, love, and live. But your identity can become distorted by others' assumptions or outdated roles. Sovereignty begins when you reclaim the authority to define yourself. This chapter invites you to stop performing and start embodying who you truly are.

Reflect

Who you believe yourself to be, consciously or unconsciously, influences every interaction, every boundary, every choice. Ask what stories you're still living by, and which ones you're ready to rewrite.

- How do you currently see yourself, in thought and in action?

____

____

____

____

____

____

____

- What do you genuinely love about how you present yourself in the world?

____

____

____

____

- What parts of you are ready to evolve into a higher expression?

____

____

____

____

Journaling Prompt: *Have I ever been misjudged?*

____

____

____

____

What did that experience teach me about expressing my truth and protecting my peace?

____

____

____

____

Reframe

You are not here to be everything to everyone. You are here to be a living embodiment of your values and your vision. Your identity isn't fixed, it's evolving. Sovereignty is the conscious shaping of that process.

- You are not defined by others' assumptions. You are defined by your alignment.

- Instead of asking, "How am I being seen?" Ask, "How do I want others to feel in my presence?"

____

____

____

____

- Reframe your identity as a living expression of your values, your voice, and your soul's vision.

Empowering Question: *What version of myself am I ready to embody more consistently with clarity, confidence, and grace?*

____

____

____

____

Reconnect

Sovereignty thrives in reflections. Who are the people that reflect your highest truths, not your smallest fears. Choose those mirrors wisely. Choose to see yourself clearly.

- **Discern Your Circle**
  – Who mirrors your highest self?

Who distorts it?

  – Express gratitude to those who uplift and empower you.
  – Create boundaries where energy is false, or constricting.

- **Fortify Yourself in Authenticity**
  – Allow your self-perception be shaped by your soul
  – Speak your truth.
  – Walk with presence.
  – Be the woman your younger self would admire.

Affirmation: *I define who I am. I live in truth, speak with grace, and align my perception with my soul's reality.*

Notes:

IDENTITY CRISIS TO IDENTITY CREATION

"Lose who you are perceived
to be so you can become
who you want to be."
~ Matthew McConaughey

Reclaiming Your Identity

Over time, life assigns us names, roles, and labels. Some empower. Others confine. Sovereign identity begins when you stop living by default and start defining yourself. This chapter invites you to peel back layers of external expectation and return to who you were and who you are.

Reflect

What various identities have you worn? Which ones have you outgrown? To reclaim who you are, first acknowledge who you are not. Identity is not a fixed story. It's your soul's evolution.

- What labels, roles, or titles have shaped how others perceive you?

____

____

____

____

____

- Do those fit who you are becoming, or are they holding you back?

____

____

____

____

- What aspects of your present identity have you outgrown?

____

____

____

____

Journaling Prompt: *What have I outgrown and what within me is quietly asking to rise?*

____

____

____

____

____

Reframe

Reframing isn't about pretending to be someone new. It's removing what's no longer true so your real self can shine forth.

- You are not defined by who you've been. You are defined by who you *choose* to become.

- If you were to "rebrand" your identity today, what

values and qualities would you lead with?

____

____

____

____

- This is not reinvention; it's a return. A remembering. A re-anchoring.

Empowering Thought: *Identity isn't fixed; it's a living expression of truth, clarity, and intention.*

Reconnect

The goal is not perfection. It's congruence. To show up in a way that feels true. The more you embody your essence, the less you need approval and the more your life reflects your Sovereignty.

- **Envision Your Fully Expressed Self**
  – What would it look and feel like to live as your boldest, most authentic self, starting now?

____

____

____

____

  – How would you walk?

____

____

____

– What would you say yes to?

____

____

____

____

– What would you release?

____

____

____

- **Radiate That Version of You Today**
  – Let your language reflect your new self.
  – Let your actions mirror your clarity.
  – Let your energy signal your change.

- You are not who the world says you are. You are who you choose to become.

Affirmation: *I am not who the world says I am. I am who I choose to become. I release outdated roles and reclaim my Sovereign identity, whole, bold, and free.*

Notes:

____

____

____

____

____

JUDGMENT TO JUDGMENT DETOX

> *"Judgment is the number*
> *one reason we feel blocked,*
> *sad, and alone. Our culture*
> *places enormous value on*
> *social status, appearance,*
> *race, religion, and material*
> *wealth. We are made to*
> *feel less than, separate, and*
> *not good enough. To protect*
> *ourselves from feeling inadequate,*
> *insecure, or unworthy, we*
> *turn to judgment."*
> *~ Gabrielle Bernstein*

Clearing the Lens of the Heart

Judgment is a disguise, a shield we use to avoid deeper pain, insecurity, or disconnection. But it doesn't protect us. It separates us.

Sovereignty invites you to do the radical, tender work of choosing compassion. It's not because others deserve it. It's because you do.

Reflect

Reflection allows you to observe your judgments without shame. Judgment is a teacher if you're willing to listen. When you trace it back, you find a place in yourself that is still healing, still longing, or still afraid.

- Who have I recently judged, and why?

____

____

____

____

- Was it their success, appearance, lifestyle, beliefs, or behavior?

____

____

____

____

- What deeper emotion might be fueling that judgment? Jealousy, fear, rejection, comparison, feeling unseen?

____

____

____

____

- Whom do I feel judged by?

____

____

____

____

- How has that shaped my self-perception or behavior?

Journaling Prompt: *What is judgment trying to protect me from and what would it take to face that with love instead?*

Reframe

- Reframing invites you to soften your judgmental gaze. You can see yourself and others more clearly.

- What if judgment became a cue for compassion, toward others and toward yourself?

- What would shift if you viewed life through love instead of fear?

Empowering Thought: *Choosing compassion is not condoning behavior; it's freeing yourself from the burden of blame.*

Reconnect

Reconnection is the healing act of seeing through softer eyes, first inward and then outward. When you release judgment, you create space for empathy, intimacy, and grace to return. Start with yourself and go from there.

- **Practice Softening Your Gaze**
  - Pause when a judgmental thought arises.
  - What pain, fear, or need might this thought be masking?
  - Replace it with curiosity or understanding.

- **Forgive Yourself and Others**
  - Write a note of release.
  - Say aloud: "I release this story. I choose peace."

- **Start Small**
  - Replace one critical thought or comment with a compassionate one, even silently.
  - Notice how your energy shifts.

Affirmation: *I release judgment and choose compassion. I see myself and others through the eyes of love. I am free to heal.*

Notes:

____

____

____

____

SEEKING HAPPINESS TO BEING HAPPINESS

*"If you want to live a
happy life, tie it to a goal,
not people or things."*
~ *Albert Einstein*

Becoming the Source of Your Joy

Too often we postpone happiness pending the next accomplishment, whether it's a promotion at work or a romantic partnership. Real joy lives in your ability to honor what's already good. This chapter invites you to stop chasing happiness and start embodying it from the inside out.

Reflect

Reflection is how you gently discover where you've been outsourcing your joy, placing it in someone else's hands or tying it to future outcomes. You don't need to judge those detours, just witness them. Then begin returning joy to its rightful place within you.

- Where are you still expecting someone or something to "make you happy"?

____

____

____

____

____

____

- Have you outsourced your joy to some future version of your life or yourself?

____

____

____

____

- When was the last time you felt truly happy? What was taking place at that moment?

____

____

____

____

Journaling Prompt: *What does happiness actually feel like in my body? Calm? Lightness? Energy? Playfulness?*

____

____

____

____

____

Reframe

Reframing helps you reclaim joy as an inside job. You don't need to earn it. You don't need to wait for it. It is available now through gratitude, intention, and presence. Your joy is not a product of perfection. It's a practice of perspective.

- Happiness isn't something to chase, it's something to choose and cultivate.

- Gratitude is the gateway. It anchors you in what's already beautiful.

- What small, present-moment joys already exist in your day. How can you invite more of them?

____

____

____

____

- Sometimes protecting your joy means protecting your peace. What boundaries need to be set, strengthened, or honored?

____

____

____

____

Empowering Thought: *You don't have to wait for happiness you can become the space that holds it.*

Reconnect

Reconnection is the act of practicing joy right now and right here. In real time. In your body. In your breath. In your laughter. The more you practice joy, the more your nervous system remembers it as home.

- **Practice Embodying Joy**
  - Savor a morning ritual: tea, light, music, stillness

– Pause for simple gratitude: one breath or one thank you
– Move your body with presence walk, stretch, dance. Let joy be in the "now," not in the "next."

- **Embody Joy as a Rhythm, Not a Reward**
  – You are not waiting for a reason.
  – You are choosing a rhythm that supports your wholeness.

Affirmation: *I am the source of my joy. I choose happiness. I radiate peace, gratitude, and love, because that is who I am.*

Notes:

____

____

____

____

____

____

____

____

____

____

____

BLIND TO SEEING

*"Change the way you look
at things, and the things
you look at will change."*
~ *Dr. Wayne Dyer*

Finding Beauty That Was Always There

Life's most sacred moments often whisper, they don't shout. But when your awareness softens, beauty begins to reveal itself everywhere: in shadows, in silence, in small gestures. This chapter invites you to trade distraction for devotion, and to find the extraordinary not by changing your life, but by seeing it differently.

Reflect

When you're overwhelmed, stressed, or chasing "something more," you miss the miracle of what already is..

- Where is your vision currently clouded? By stress or by routine? By expectation or by disappointment?

____

____

____

____

____

____

- When was the last time you noticed beauty in something ordinary? Light through a window, laughter, or a simple meal?

____

____

____

____

- What emotions or thoughts color how you see the world during challenging moments?

____

____

____

____

- Are you truly open to finding beauty even in discomfort or simplicity?

____

____

____

____

Journaling Prompt: *What area of my life feels dull or frustrating and how might I reframe it as sacred or beautiful?*

____

____

____

____

Reframe

Reframing invites you to shift your inner dialogue and change how you interpret your environment. Beauty is not reserved for perfect days. It lives in imperfection, in pause, in perspective. Wonder becomes available the moment you decide to meet the world with new eyes.

- Shift your perspective and let *wonder* replace weariness.

- **Try this new inner dialogue**
  - Instead of "This traffic is wasting my time," say: "This is an invitation to pause and breathe."
  - Instead of "Nothing special is happening," say: "Today is filled with moments I've never experienced before."

- Empower your perception by choosing a lens that honors presence and possibility.

Empowering Question: *How can I begin to see the sacred in what I've been overlooking?*

____

____

____

____

Reconnect

Reconnection means returning to the present with your body, your breath, and all your senses. Beauty doesn't hide. It waits to be seen. When you tune into the details of life, even the mundane becomes meaningful.

- **Practice Open-Eye Meditation**
  Wherever you are, car, kitchen, desk, garden:

– Take a slow, grounding breath
– Gently scan your space
– Let your eyes rest on one detail
– Observe it deeply. Let it tell a story.
– Ask Yourself: "What is this moment awakening in me?"

____

____

____

____

- **Create Beauty Awareness Prompts**
  – What are three "window seat" moments to create this week?

____

____

____

  – Where can you soften your gaze and see with new eyes?

____

____

____

  – What would shift if you treated ordinary moments like sacred invitations?

____

____

____

Affirmation: *I choose to see clearly. I soften into the present moment. Beauty surrounds me, because I choose to see it.*

WEARING CLOTHES TO CURATING A SIGNATURE LOOK

*"Dress shabbily, and they
remember the dress;
dress impeccably, and
they remember the woman."*
~ Coco Chanel

Style as a Statement of Sovereignty

Style isn't shallow, it's soulful. What you wear tells the world who you are, what you value, and how you carry your power. Your appearance shouldn't be about conformity or consumption. It's about clarity. Step into your closet to curate your expression and to wear your worth boldly and beautifully.

Reflect

Reflection helps you examine the unconscious ways you've been dressing for acceptance, comfort, or invisibility. Reflection invites you to shift toward expression, alignment, and expansion. Your clothes tell a story. What story are they telling?

____

____

____

____

____

- When you look in the mirror, do you see a woman who reflects your inner essence?

____

____

- Does your wardrobe support or suppress the version you're stepping into?

____

____

- When do you feel most alive in your clothing? When do you tend to hide?

____

____

____

____

Journaling Prompts: *What three words do I want my appearance to communicate?*

____

____

____

____

What pieces in my current wardrobe reflect who I am becoming?

____

____

____

How do I want to feel when I get dressed?

Reframe

Treat style not as vanity, but as a vehicle of visibility. When you dress with intention, you embody your energy before you speak. Style becomes a sacred ritual, an external sign of your inner evolution.

- Style is power in motion.

- Your signature look is an outward affirmation of internal truth.

- Getting dressed should be a ritual of identity and intention.

- Your clothes can mute you or amplify you. Choose to be amplified.

Empowering Thought: *Style isn't about impressing others. It's about expressing yourself with clarity, confidence, and grace.*

Reconnect

Fashion reconnection means expressing yourself boldly, consciously, and creatively. It isn't about trend-chasing, it's about truth-wearing. When your external reflection embodies your internal, alignment deepens, and the world begins to recognize your presence before you speak.

- **Start Small, Start Strong**
  Choose one intentional outfit this week that reflects your future self. Ask: "Does this express who I am becoming?"

____

____

- **Choose a Power Piece**
  – A fitted blazer, a bold lipstick color, a silky scarf, a necklace, something that feels like your Crown.
  – Let it anchor your energy and elevate your presence.

- **Create a "Look & Feel" Board**
  – Use Pinterest, a journal, or a wall collage to gather visual inspiration.
  – Use references that reflect your energy, not just your body.
  – Follow a fashion brand on Instagram that reflects your aspirational style, and when needed, seek out a more accessible piece that offers the same feeling and expression.

- **Mirror Practice**
  – Stand in front of the mirror. Hold your gaze.
  – Ask Yourself: "Do I look like someone who knows her worth?"

____

____

Affirmation: *I wear my truth. I move with grace. I embody my power with one look, one choice, one day at a time.*

Part Three

MANIFESTATION

IGNITE YOUR DREAMS, ALIGN YOUR PATH & EMBODY YOUR DESTINY

MANIFESTING FROM NEPTUNE IN PISCES TO NEPTUNE IN ARIES

*"The secret of getting
ahead is getting started."*
~ Mark Twain

Igniting Desire into Action

Aries energy is bold, unapologetic, and instinct-driven. It doesn't wait for permission, it moves. This chapter invites you to activate your desires with the fire of Aries energy through clarity, courage, and aligned action. No more waiting for the right time. Now is sacred. Now is Sovereign.

Reflect

Reflection invites you to locate the dreams you've placed on the back burner. Dreams you told yourself you'll pursue when you're more ready, more qualified, more sure. But true creation doesn't begin with certainty. It begins with desire and decision. Desire is the divine spark of decision. Are you honoring it or hiding it?

- What dreams or desires have you delayed, waiting for timing, approval, or proof?

____

____

____

____

- Where have you been hoping life will shift instead of consciously shaping it?

____

____

____

- When you think about full ownership of your path, your time, your power and your destiny, do you feel fear or freedom?

____

____

____

Journaling Prompt: *What have I been waiting to begin?*

____

____

____

____

____

How would it feel to stop waiting?

____

____

____

Reframe

Manifestation is not a wish. It's a willingness to trust your inspiration. To act before you're certain. To move before you're validated. Aries energy initiates. Your deepest desires don't need perfection. They need motion.

- You are not unprepared. You are in progress. You are becoming.

- Manifestation means engagement. It's showing up. It's doing the next brave thing.

- Readiness is not a prerequisite. You don't need to feel ready. You need to get started.

Mantra: *I manifest through movement. My soul leads. I follow.*

Reconnect

Aries charges forward. Its energy reminds you that every step is a sacred flame. Self-initiation is your birthright. Action aligns your internal fire with external form.

- **Name Your Desire Out Loud**
  Write it down. Speak it. Claim the dream you've been whispering inside. Let it echo outside of you.

____

____

____

____

____

- **Take One Tangible Step**
  - Make the call
  - Sign up for the class.
  - Send the email.
  - Invest. Inquire. Initiate.

- **Start a Morning Mantra Practice**
  Each day, say: "I manifest through movement. My soul leads. I follow."

- **Celebrate Progress, Not Perfection**
  Every step is momentum. Every action is an offering. Aries reminds you: forward is enough.

Affirmation: *I was born to begin. I was born to blaze. My dreams are divine and I move with purpose.*

Notes:

____

____

____

____

____

____

____

____

____

LIMITED BELIEFS TO LIMITLESS POSSIBILITIES

"We all get what we tolerate.
Stop tolerating excuses
within yourself, limiting
beliefs of the past, or
half-assed fearful states."
~ Tony Robbins

Freeing Yourself From the Limits You Inherited

Possibility begins where old beliefs end. Many perceptions are not personal truths. They are inherited scripts, shaped by fear, culture, or conditioning. So question what you've accepted, rewrite what you've been told, and awaken to the truth. The life you crave is possible and it starts with what you believe.

Reflect

Reflection is where liberation starts. Before you expand, you must reflect on the stories that have shaped your sense of what's possible. When you pause and find the script that's holding you back, you gain the power to rewrite it.

- What beliefs did you inherit about success, love, money, creativity, or worth? Start to question them.

- Whose voice echoes in your mind when you second-guess yourself?

____

____

____

____

- Where do you feel stuck right now? What belief keeps you there?

____

____

____

____

Journaling Prompt: *What have I believed about myself that no longer feels true and what am I ready to believe instead?*

____

____

____

____

Reframe

Reframing gives you the freedom to choose again. What you inherited isn't what you have to keep. Every belief is a doorway. You can choose whether to walk through it or build a new one. If someone else has done what you dream of, it means the path exists. If no one has, it means you are the pioneer. Say:

- "This isn't my belief, it was handed to me. I can choose a new one."

- "If someone has done what I dream of doing, it means I can too."
- "My potential is far greater than the limits I've been taught to accept."

Mantra: *I am not bound by belief. I choose what expands me.*

Reconnect

Reconnection is the practice of building your life by intentionally choosing new beliefs, embodying them. You surround yourself with mirrors that reflect your possibilities, not your limitations.

- **Rewrite the Story**
  Identify one limiting belief. Then replace it with a liberating truth:
  – Limiting: "I was not meant to lead."
  – Liberating: "I was born to rise and guide from my heart."

____

____

____

____

____

____

____

____

- **Speak It Daily**
  Say your new belief out loud each morning. Speak it like a vow. Let your body feel it.

- **Surround Yourself With Possibility**
  Seek mentors, communities, and friendships that stretch you. Be around those who live in expansion not fear.

- **Follow the Evidence**
  Find stories of people who've defied their past, their doubt, their odds. Let their courage ignite your own.

Affirmation: *I release the beliefs that confined me. I step into a life defined by truth, courage, and limitless possibility.*

Notes:

____

____

____

____

____

____

____

____

____

____

DREAMER TO DOER

"Dreams are lovely, but
they are just dreams.
Dreams don't come true
because you dream them.
It's hard work that
creates change."
~ *Shonda Rhimes*

Someday Is Now

Dreams are not meant to remain in the realm of imagination. They are meant to be lived. Too often we confuse preparation with progress. We wait for permission but we can only give that to ourselves. You need to stop circling your calling and start walking toward it. Boldly. Imperfectly. Now.

Reflect

Reflection means re-naming the dreams you've called "timing" or "readiness." Sometimes what holds us back isn't fear of failure, it's fear of finally beginning.

- What vision or desire have you carried in your heart for years, even decades?

____

____

____

____

- Have you been mistaking research, planning, or talking about the dream as progress without taking real action?

____

____

____

____

- Where are you still waiting for someone else's validation or approval?

____

____

____

____

Journaling Prompt: *What dream keeps calling me and what has kept me from answering until now?*

____

____

____

____

Reframe

Reframing invites you to see that you are not late, now you're aligned. You're not unprepared, now you're in motion. Dreams are made real not by perfect timing, but by consistent action. Readiness is not a feeling. It's a decision to begin ready or not.

- You're not behind. You're on the edge of a breakthrough.

- It isn't about being ready. It's about being willing.

- One small action today is worth more than a perfect plan tomorrow.

Mantra: *I move forward, not because I have it all figured out, but because I refuse to wait any longer.*

Reconnect

Reconnection is the sacred act of aligning your values with your calendar. Dreams manifest not through old hopes but through new habits. The shift happens when you stop saying "someday" and start building something today.

- **Choose One Dream You've Delayed**
  Name it. Honor it. No matter how big or far off it feels, choose this as your starting point.

____

____

____

____

- **Write Down Why It Matters**
  Why is this dream important to you? What will it unlock?

____

____

____

____

- Who might it impact beyond yourself?

____

____

____

____

- **Schedule the Very Next Step**
  – Enroll in the class. Send the email. Research the next step.
  – Make time to write, record, build, and move.

- **Speak It Aloud**
  Stand tall and say: "I am doing this not someday, but now." Let your body believe it. Let your spirit respond.

Affirmation: *I no longer wait for the perfect moment. I act on what matters. My dreams move through me into the world now.*

Notes:

____

____

____

____

____

____

____

____

WANDERING TO WANDERLUST

"Not all who wander are lost"
~ J.R.R. Tolkien

Take the Sacred Journey Back to You

The most transformative journeys don't always require a passport. A sacred pause, an intentional day, or even an afternoon alone can reconnect you to your essence. You step away from productivity long enough to remember who you are beneath the noise. This is your permission to wander, not to escape, but to return to yourself.

Reflect

Reflection means checking in with the part of you that doesn't speak in tasks or to-do lists. When was the last time you traveled not outward, but inward? Often what you crave most isn't more stimulation, but space to feel, to dream, and to hear your own inner voice again.

- What does your soul need most right now: stillness, adventure, reconnection, or reimagination?

____

____

____

____

____

- When was the last time you traveled or took space with no agenda other than to feel more like yourself?

____

____

____

- Have you allowed yourself the kind of pause that nourishes your spirit, not just your schedule?

____

____

____

Journaling Prompt: *What part of me is longing to be heard and what kind of journey will help me hear it?*

____

____

____

Reframe

Reframing reminds you that intentional solitude is sacred. In a world that praises output, creating time to be with your own being is an act of power.

- You don't need a major trip. You need a soul-led moment that says: "This is for me. This is for now."

- You don't need a plane ticket or a month-long escape. You need an intentional pause.

- "Wandering" isn't being lost, it's being open. Open to stillness. Open to clarity. Open to rediscovery.

Mantra: *I don't need to escape my life. I just need to return to myself.*

Reconnect

Reconnection is about giving your soul the space it's been whispering for. Whether it's an afternoon in nature, a solo retreat, or a silent morning by candlelight, these pauses restore your inner compass. You don't have to go far to come home to yourself.

- **Create a Wanderlust fund**
  - Open a small savings account or envelope.
  - Contribute consistently, even if it's $5/week.
  - Intention builds momentum.

- **Choose a Local Escape**
  Book a retreat, attend a workshop, visit a museum solo, or spend a night alone in nature or a quiet Airbnb.

- **Walk, Wander, and Listen**
  Take your journal and go somewhere new: a forest trail, a riverside, an overlook. Let your environment speak. Let your soul respond.

- **Treat Time With Yourself as Sacred**
  Light a candle. Brew tea slowly. Journal with presence. Let your rituals remind you: I am worthy of this time.

Affirmation: *I travel within to remember who I am. My presence is my power. My soul leads me home.*

Notes:

PERFECTION TO PASSION

"Passion drives perfection."
~ Rick Warren

Keep the Flame of Passion Burning without Burning Out

Passion is sacred fuel. But without boundaries it can become a wildfire. People burn out when they chase perfection or approval instead of honoring flow. Keep your fire alive with presence, not pressure. You don't need to be flawless to make a difference. You just need to stay lit from within.

Reflect

Reflection invites you to notice where your passion may have been replaced by performance. Are you showing up with soul, or trying to control how you're seen? Rather than perfection, passion demands the kind of permission that comes from you, not others.

- Where in your life are you clinging to perfection out of fear of judgment, failure, or being "not enough"?

- What passion, idea, or creative spark would you begin today if you didn't feel the need to do it flawlessly?

____

____

____

____

- When was the last time you felt fully lit up by something and what stopped you from following that feeling?

____

____

____

____

Journaling Prompt: *What would I dare to begin if I let myself be messy, honest, and fully alive?*

____

____

____

____

____

Reframe

- Passion-based mistakes don't mean you're off track. They're signs you're moving. You don't have to be perfect to be powerful. You have to be true.

- Passion isn't sloppy, it's sincere. It's your soul in motion.

- Your impact doesn't come from how polished you are. It comes from how present you are.

Mantra: *My fire doesn't need to be perfect. It just needs to be real.*

Reconnect

Reconnection is the practice of choosing aligned action over delayed perfection. Passion lives small steps, shared sparks, honest expression. Take care of your inner fire. Tend it with joy, not pressure. Let it warm others without consuming yourself.

- **Write Down Three Things That Light You Up**
  Think of what makes you feel alive, even if it scares you. Especially if it scares you.

____

____

____

- **Take One Brave Step Toward One of Them**
  – Make the call.
  – Sign up for the class.
  – Write the first page
  – Speak the idea aloud.

- **Let Yourself Be Seen**
  Share your passion with someone you trust. Not your resume. Your real version. Let them see the spark, not the script.

Affirmation: *I tend to my fire with care. I move with joy, not pressure. My passion is my power and it lights the way.*

Notes:

____

____

____

____

____

____

____

____

____

____

____

____

____

____

____

LOSS TO GRATITUDE

*"The more we give thanks, the
more we receive to be thankful
for. Gratitude is the gift
that always gives back."
~ Matthew McConaughey*

Turning Grief Into Gratitude

Loss leaves a mark but it can also leave meaning.
Gratitude doesn't erase grief, but it reshapes the way
we hold it. This chapter is an invitation to explore how
deep sorrow can coexist with sacred remembering.
Gratitude becomes the thread that gently weaves pain
into purpose, and absence into deeper presence.

Reflect

Sit honestly with your grief, not to fix it, but to face
it with tenderness. Sometimes what lingers is not just
sadness. It's love that has nowhere to go. By revisiting
loss through a lens of appreciation, you begin to see
that even in the end something beautiful can remain.

- What is one loss that brings grief in you, whether
  new or long buried?

- What part of that experience still lives in you: as a value, a memory, a lesson, or a sense of who you've become?

____

____

____

____

- How might you honor the love and meaning that remains, even with the absence?

____

____

____

____

Journaling Prompt: *What did this loss teach me about love, life, or presence and how can I live in honor of it today?*

____

____

____

____

Reframe

Reframing allows you to see that gratitude allows grief some space to breathe. You're not being asked to be thankful for the pain, but to be thankful through it. The most difficult chapters in our lives often contain the deepest invitations into wisdom, compassion, and clarity.

- Gratitude doesn't ignore grief, it softens grief.

- Every goodbye carries a hidden blessing waiting to be acknowledged and lived forward.

- What if the most painful parts of your story are the most sacred, because of how they shaped you?

Mantra: *I hold my sorrow in one hand and my gratitude in the other. Both are true. Both are holy.*

Reconnect

The recipients of your gratitude are not just a list. They're a lens. As you remember what shaped you, grief looks less like a burden and more like a bridge.

- **Start a Daily Gratitude Ritual**
  Keep it simple: each morning, write down 3–5 things you're grateful for: people, sensations, comforts, insights.

- **Write a Letter of Thanks**
  Choose someone who shaped you, even if they're no longer living. Write to them. Speak the gratitude you never got to express.

- **Bless the Ordinary**
  Choose one simple item in your life and bless it each day. Let it become a moment of sacred appreciation.

Affirmation: *I carry my grief with grace. I honor what was, and give thanks for what remains. In gratitude, I heal.*

Notes:

SCARCITY TO ABUNDANCE

> *"Acknowledging the good*
> *that you already have in*
> *your life is the foundation*
> *for all abundance."*
>
> ~ *Eckhart Tolle*

Cultivating Scarcity to Sacred Plenty

Scarcity begins in the mind, not the bank account or calendar. It's shaped by fear, comparison, and conditioning. Abundance is not something you chase. It's something you choose to see, feel, and embody.

Reflect

Scarcity doesn't always mean absence. Sometimes it's disconnection: from presence, from trust, from the truth that abundance already exists within and around you.

- Where are you currently experiencing scarcity? In time, love, money, creativity, opportunity?

____

____

____

____

____

____

- What story are you telling yourself about what's missing?

____

____

____

____

- Is this story rooted in fact? Or in fear, comparison, or old conditioning?

____

____

____

____

____

Journaling Prompt: *What would shift if I stopped focusing on what I don't have and started blessing what I do?*

____

____

____

____

Reframe

Reframing allows you to see that lack is not always reality; it's often perception. What you focus on multiplies. When you choose gratitude, you amplify awareness. And where there is awareness, there is abundance waiting to be received.

- Lack is a feeling, not a fact. Feelings can change with perspective.

- What you bless, grows. What you resent, repels.

- When you honor what already exists, that energy attracts what's aligned.

Mantra: *I live in the flow of enough. What I seek is already seeking me.*

Reconnect

Reconnection is about turning your attention from fear to faith and aligning your energy with the abundance you desire. It isn't about pretending. It's about embodying as if you are already resourced, already connected, already free. Because in many ways you are.

- **Visualize Your Expansion**
  Choose one area of scarcity. Close your eyes and imagine that part of your life is already full. Feel it. Breathe it. Let all your systems register it as real.

- **Celebrate Abundance in Others**
  When you see someone really thriving, celebrate them. Their gain is not your loss. Let their success stretch your capacity to receive.

- **Practice "As If"**
  Move, speak, and make decisions from your abundant self. Dress like it. Walk like it. Choose with confidence. Show the universe you're already living aligned with what you're calling in.

Affirmation: *I release the story of not enough. I am deeply supported. I am already in abundance and it continues to grow.*

Notes:

CLUTTERED MIND TO LASER-FOCUSED DESIRE

*"When you really want something,
the universe conspires to
help you to achieve it."*
~ *Paulo Coelho*

Focus on How You Want to Feel

We're taught to chase titles, timelines, outcomes. But behind every desire is a deeper longing: to feel a certain way. When you clarify the feeling beneath the goal, you align with your truth, not just your to-do list.

Reflect

Reflection invites you to question what you're working toward. It's a mistake to pursue goals shaped by others' values. When you know how you actually want to feel, the path forward becomes more honest and more alive.

- What do you really want right now, in your career, your relationships, health, and in your self-expression?

____

____

____

____

____

____

- Is it rooted in who you are or who you think you should be?

____

____

____

- Are your goals based on external standards or internal resonance?

____

____

____

- Beneath the surface of what you want, what feeling are you after?

____

____

____

Journaling Prompt: *If I could feel anything without earning it what would I choose?*

____

____

____

____

Reframe

You don't need all the answers. You do need emotional clarity. When you understand how you want to feel, your decisions shift from wanting to receiving. You become a magnet for experiences that reflect your truth.

- You don't need the whole plan. You just need to know how you want to feel.

- Perfection isn't the point, resonance is.

- Clarity doesn't come from thinking harder. It comes from moving with intention and adjusting as you go.

Mantra: *I lead with how I want to feel. My desires are rooted in truth, not performance.*

Reconnect

Get back to your emotional compass, the inner knowing that tells you what is aligned, expansive, and true. When you understand the feeling you're chasing and live as if it's already available, you shift your energy from longing to embodiment.

- **Choose One Core Desire**
  Write it down, then ask:
  - "Why do I want this?"
  - "What feeling am I really after?"

- **Take One Aligned Action Today**
  It can be a phone call, a wardrobe change, or a boundary reset. Let it be in service of a feeling , not just the goal.

- **Create a Vision Around the Feeling**
  – Make a mini vision board or journal entry based on that emotion, not the outcome.
  – Let the feeling shape your visuals and words: calm, excitement, freedom, presence and love.

Affirmation: *I honor how I want to feel. I choose aligned action over approval. My desires are sacred, and they begin with me.*

Notes:

____

____

____

____

____

____

____

____

____

____

____

____

DISTRACTION TO INTENTIONAL ACTION

*"The 5 Second Rule: The moment you
have an instinct to act on a goal
you must 5-4-3-2-1 and physically
move or your brain will stop you."*
~ Mel Robbins

Claiming the Day Before It Claims You

Your day doesn't begin when the alarm goes off, it begins when your attention is focused. The choices you make, especially in the early moments, either align you with purpose or reactively scatter your thoughts in reaction. You need to shift from autopilot to intention, from distraction to devotion. You don't need more hours in your day. You need more alignment with what matters.

Reflect

Reflection helps you notice where your time, focus, and energy are flowing. Presence is a practice. Mindful ownership of your day starts with one honest check-in at a time.

- Do you begin your day with intention or do you immediately react to outside demands?

____

____

____

____

- What are your most frequent distractions?

____

____

____

____

- What do they cost you mentally, emotionally, and energetically?

____

____

____

____

- When during your day do you naturally feel most focused, energized, and clear?

____

____

____

____

Journaling Prompt: *If I were to honor what matters most, how would I shape the first hour of my day?*

____

____

____

____

____

Reframe

Stop labeling yourself as "unfocused" or "all over the place." Proactive discipline rooted in desire and devotion becomes freedom. Clarity without hustle is equal to productivity.

- You're not "bad at focus." You've simply been stretched in too many directions without a sacred anchor.

- Discipline isn't about force, it's about devotion to what deeply matters.

- You don't need more time, you need more clarity about what deserves your attention.

Mantra: *My presence is powerful. My day is shaped by what I choose to honor.*

Reconnect

Reconnection is about aligning action with intention every day. When you pause to choose what matters before the day chooses for you, you regain your Sovereignty. Even small shifts create big momentum.

- **Set Tomorrow in Motion Tonight**
  Before bed, write down your top three priorities for the next day. Let clarity arrive before the chaos.

- **Taking Action** (*The 5 Second Rule*)
  Upon waking up, instead of lying in bed and obsessing about a topic, count down 5-4-3-2-1 and physically move your body out of bed before the five seconds are up.

- **Protect the First Hour**
  – Keep your phone on airplane mode.

– Light a candle, breathe, stretch, journal, or simply sit with your thoughts.
– Let your energy lead, not your notifications.

- **Devote 15 Uninterrupted Minutes**
  Choose the one task or dream you've been avoiding. Set a timer and begin. Just the act getting started shifts your momentum.

Affirmation: *I honor my energy by choosing with intention. Each mindful act shapes a life I am proud to live.*

Notes:

____

____

____

____

____

____

____

____

____

____

OBSESSION WITH AN IDEA TO PLANTING THE SEED OF DESIRE

*"Desires are seeds waiting
for their season to sprout.
From a single seed of desire,
whole forests grow."*

~ Deepak Chopra

Planting a Seed and Letting It Bloom in Its Own Time

Every desire is a seed. But growth takes patience, presence, and trust. Too often we try to force results, mistaking urgency for faith. You are not here to control every outcome. You are here to co-create with grace.

Reflect

Reflection invites you to acknowledge the desire that's been quietly within you, maybe for years. Has it been nurtured with care, or afflicted with tension? True manifestation begins with listening and patience.

- What is one deep desire you've carried in your heart for years without letting go?

____

____

____

____

____

- Have you been gently nurturing this desire, or anxiously obsessing over it?

____

____

____

____

- Can you remember a moment when life surprised you with something far better than what you were trying to control?

____

____

____

____

Journaling Prompt: *What desire am I ready to trust again not with pressure, but with patience and presence?*

____

____

____

____

____

____

Reframe

When you release the need to control the "how" and "when," you begin to walk in alignment instead of anxiety. Clarity invites. Desperation repels. Growth needs space.

- Desire is magnetic. Desperation is resistant.

- You don't have to chase. You only need to clarify your vision, align your actions, and trust the unfolding.

- Let go of controlling the how and when. Let life co-author the journey. Let it delight you.

Mantra: *I plant the seed in trust. I water it with presence. I release the timeline.*

Reconnect

Tend to your desires like a gardener. You do your part and then allow the sun, soil, and seasons to do theirs. You don't manifest through force. You manifest through alignment, belief, and daily acts of faith.

- **Revisit One Core Desire**
  Ask Yourself: "How does this desire serve your highest good and the good of others?"

- **Live in the Energy of Already Having It**
  Embody the outcome before it arrives. Dress for it. Speak from it. Make choices aligned with your future self.

- **Surround Yourself With Expansive Energy**
  Be with people who stretch your thinking, support your vision, and remind you what's possible, not just what's practical.

Affirmation: *My desires are seeds of destiny. I plant with intention, water with love, and trust what will bloom.*

Notes:

____

____

____

____

____

____

____

____

____

____

____

____

____

____

RESISTANCE TO PERSISTENCE

"Persistence overcomes resistance."
~ Mark Victor Hansen

The Power of Gentle Devotion

Persistence isn't always loud or forceful. Often it's quiet, rhythmic, and rooted. In a world that glorifies immediate results, it's easy to misread delays as denials. Soul-led goals require a different pace. So shift from resistance to rhythm. Choose steady devotion over self-doubt. What's meant for you responds to your consistency, not your control.

Reflect

When have you expected results to come quickly and then abandoned the process when they didn't? Lasting growth is built in seasons, not sprints.

- Where in your life have you mistaken delay for denial?

____

____

____

____

- Do you give up if results don't arrive quickly or do you trust the long game?

____

____

____

- What vision, project, or dream in your life right now deserves more of your presence and persistence?

____

____

____

Journaling Prompt: *Where am I being asked to stay the course, not with pressure, but with presence?*

____

____

____

____

____

____

____

____

____

Reframe

Resistance isn't a red light, it's a request to reframe and realign. Every dream worth having requires moments of waiting, recalibrating, and trusting. When you show up consistently, even imperfectly. you prove your faith to the dream itself.

- Resistance is not a stop sign, its a signal to return to alignment.

- Your dream is not too big. Your timeline is not too late.

- Progress isn't about doing it all today. It's about moving forward.

Mantra: *I am devoted, not desperate. I move forward, one aligned step at a time.*

Reconnect

Reconnection is the practice of persistently staying connected to your vision. You don't have to force the outcome. You only have to keep showing up. The effects of small, daily actions are immensely powerful. That's how momentum begins and continues.

- **Dedicate 15 Minutes Each Morning to Your Vision**
  Visualize, sketch, plan, take action. The habit creates the path.

- **Replace Frustration With Faith**
  Say aloud: "What I seek is also seeking me."

- **Keep Showing Up**
  You don't have to "feel like it" every day. You only have to honor the dream with your presence. Quiet devotion builds more momentum than bursts of pressure.

Affirmation: *I persist with grace. I trust the unfolding. I honor my dreams with steady love, not urgency.*

Notes:

BIRD'S EYE VIEW TO SPY PLANE VIEW

"Your attitude, not your aptitude, will determine your altitude."

~ Zig Ziglar

Elevate Your Vision and Soar High

Sometimes, the breakthrough isn't in doing more. It's seeing from a greater height. True vision comes from elevation, from rising above "what is" to discover "what could be." Elevate your altitude, shift your vantage point, and gain the clarity that comes from rising.

Reflect

Reflection asks you to examine your current "big picture." Is it truly expansive or just a bit larger than what feels safe? Have you been zooming out, but not up? Don't miss opportunities by viewing your path through old filters.

- Where are you operating from a 30,000-foot view when you could go even higher?

____

____

____

____

- Is your current "big picture" your highest self, or in past assumptions, old desires, or self-imposed limitations?

____

____

____

____

- What would become possible if you saw your life, your work, your purpose from a higher perspective?

____

____

____

____

Journaling Prompt: *What have I been viewing from the ground and what might shift if I saw it from above?*

____

____

____

____

Reframe

Reframing invites you to understand that vision is not a gift for the chosen, it's power for the committed. When you elevate your perspective, you access clarity that simply isn't available from a lower level. You recognize what matters and release what doesn't.

- 70,000 feet is not out of reach. It's a practice of stepping back, rising above, and daring to dream beyond what's visible now.

- What looks like chaos at ground level becomes coherence from above.

- The next-level vision you're waiting for isn't out of reach. It's waiting for you to rise up and meet it.

Mantra: *I rise for clarity. I lead from vision. I return grounded in purpose.*

Reconnect

You don't elevate by accident. You elevate through pause, presence, and perspective. Give yourself space to dream higher, think clearer, and return with renewed direction.

- **Create a Personal Offsite**
  – Once a month, block off a full day for seeing the whole picture. No errands. No emails. Just you, and your future.
  – Ask big questions. Let yourself imagine beyond the now.

- **Revisit a Stalled Goal**
  Ask Yourself:
  – "What would this look like from 70,000 feet?"

____

____

____

____

– "What are the patterns?"

____

____

____

– "What's the bigger opportunity?"

____

____

____

– "What would the highest version of yourself choose to do?"

____

____

____

- **Use Mantra as Meditation**
  Sit quietly and repeat: "I rise above for wisdom, and return to earth with power." Let your breath match the rhythm of your vision.

Affirmation: *I see from above, I lead with vision. I align with elevation and act with grounded grace.*

Notes:

____

____

____

PESSIMISM TO OPTIMISM

*"Optimism isn't a belief
that things will automatically
get better. It's a conviction
to make them better."*
~ Melinda French Gates

Living in the Frequency of Favor

In a world that often primes us to expect the worst, choosing to believe in the best is a revolutionary practice. So join the revolution. Expect support, invite alignment, and move through uncertainty with a spirit that knows the best outcome is unfolding.

Reflect

Optimism isn't a delusion, it's a decision. Even before the evidence is visible, it's the choice to see life through a lens of support rather than sabotage.

- What has your mind been rehearsing lately, possibility or fear?

- When did you see optimism pay off? If never, start now.

____

____

____

____

- What would shift if you expected *good news*, not just braced for impact?

____

____

____

____

Journaling Prompt: *What am I ready to believe is possible again, even if I've stopped saying it out loud?*

____

____

____

____

Reframe

You don't have to pretend everything is perfect. But you can believe that what's happening is guiding you toward something meaningful. Setbacks can redirect you. Optimism lets you hold on to the bigger picture, even when the current view seems unclear.

- Replace "What if it goes wrong?" with "What if it works out better than I imagined?"

- Setbacks are often setups. You're being positioned, not punished.

- Delay is not denial. It's an invitation to deepen trust, not diminish belief.

Mantra: *What's meant for me is already on its way and it's better than I expected.*

Reconnect

Reconnection is not just hoping things will go well. It's acting as if they already are. Optimism becomes a vibration. A practice. A lens. When you look through it consistently, life starts to respond in kind.

- **Keep a "Proof-of-Possibility" Journal**
  Each day, write down small miracles, aligned moments, unexpected kindness, or new breakthroughs. These are reminders: "Life is working with me."

- **Speak Your Desires Into Existence**
  Say them out loud. Daily. With confidence. Not begging. Believing. Your voice is a tool for alignment.

- **Use This Anchor Mantra When Doubt Creeps In**
  "I trust what is meant for me is already on its way." Repeat this before you act, and when fear begins to whisper.

Affirmation: *I live in the frequency of favor. I expect the best and I open fully to receive it.*

Notes:

NO TO A RESOUNDING *YES!*

Saying Yes to the Soul's Invitation

Not every opportunity deserves your energy, but some are sacred invitations to grow, expand, and step deeper into alignment. Knowing when to say *yes* is not about pressure or performance; it's about resonance. Accept the invitation to tune in, trust your inner knowing, and courageously respond when life offers you something that calls your name.

Reflect

Notice how your body and spirit react when something meaningful arises. A *yes* might not feel easy, but it feels alive. It hums a melody beneath the uncertainty. It's not just, "Can I do this?" Instead it's, "This moves me closer to the person I'm becoming."

- When have you felt pulled toward something, but hesitated?

____

____

____

____

____

____

- What physical sensations show up in your body when something is a true *yes*. Expansion? Warmth? Excitement?

____

____

____

____

- Can you name a time you said *yes* and it changed you? Or when saying *no* brought regret?

____

____

____

____

Journaling Prompt: *What opportunities or desires have I quietly wanted to say yes to but haven't trusted myself to claim yet?*

____

____

____

____

Reframe

Reframing allows a shift from overthinking to inner listening. A true *yes* may challenge you, but it won't betray you. The most aligned path may feel scary because it's new, not because it's wrong.

- Saying *yes* isn't about being ready. It's about being *willing.*

- A true yes might scare you, but it also excites you.

- Instead of asking "Can I do this?" ask *"Does this align with who I'm here to become?"*

Mantra: *I trust what lights me up. My yes is sacred, and I follow it with courage.*

Reconnect

When you say *yes* from truth, you activate momentum. You step into flow. You let life meet you in your willingness. Saying *yes* isn't about having the whole plan. It's about trusting the next step.

- **Revisit a Desire or Opportunity You've Been Avoiding**
  - Ask Yourself: "Is this stretching me or steering me away from myself?"

  ____

  ____

  ____

  - If it expands and excites you, move toward it.

- **Speak Your Yes Out Loud**
  Claim it. Let your voice carry your commitment. "This is for me. I say yes."

- **Support Your Yes With Aligned Action**
  - Make the call.
  - Register for the thing.

– Block time.
– Say yes with your calendar, your money, your presence.

Affirmation: *When I say yes to what aligns, life responds with clarity, courage, and grace.*

Notes:

____

____

____

____

____

____

____

____

____

____

____

____

____

RELEASE TO EXPAND

*"We must be willing to let
go of the life we've planned,
so as to have the life
that is waiting for us".*
~ *Joseph Campbell*

The Sacred Art of Letting Go

Releasing isn't weakness, it's wisdom. What once served you may now be stalling you. Letting go is not about loss. It's about seeing what's outdated, untangling from what's no longer true, and creating space for a life that fits who you're becoming, not just who you've been.

Reflect

Acknowledge what is still holding on to, and ask whether they reflect your current truth. Weight we carry isn't from what we lack, but from what we haven't yet released.

- What are you still carrying that feels like a burden?

____

____

____

____

____

____

- Is this person, pattern, belief, or role serving your current growth or binding you to a past version of yourself?

____

____

____

____

- What would you gain energetically, emotionally and spiritually if you chose to release this?

____

____

____

____

Journaling Prompt: *What am I afraid to release and what am I more afraid of missing if I don't?*

____

____

____

____

Reframe

Reframing allows you to shift your understanding of release from loss to liberation. You are not betraying your past by evolving. You are honoring your truth by clearing space. Letting go is a sacred form of self-respect.

- Releasing is not rejection. It's a redirect.
- You're not losing. you're lightening.

- Letting go isn't giving up, it's choosing aligned truth over outdated loyalty.

Mantra: *I bless what was. I honor what is. I release to rise.*

Reconnect

Reconnection is making space for new desires asking to emerge. It's also about creating ritual around the release so that it becomes conscious, embodied, and honored. When you let go with intention, you don't just push something into your past. You invite something from your future.

- **Ask What's Now Asking for Space**
  What desire, vision, or part of yourself is ready to grow, if only there were room?

____

____

____

____

- **Speak With Intention**
  Say aloud: "I am releasing XXX. I am inviting YYY and ZZZ." Let it be a vow, a personal ceremony, a blessing.

- **Honor the Grief**
  – Even letting go of what hurts can feel like a loss.
  – Make space for tears, stillness, or quiet ceremony.
  – Grief is sacred. It clears your soul for what's next.

- **Begin a Gentle Ritual of Release**
  – Write what you're letting go of and burn it (safely).

– Bury it.

____

____

____

____

– Speak it out loud and bless it.
– Move your body to release stored energy.

- **Envision the New**
  What will feel lighter? Freer? More joyful? Plant that seed today.

____

____

____

____

- **Practice Radical Self-Compassion**
  – Growth isn't linear. Be gentle with yourself.
  – Releasing takes courage. Integration takes time.

Affirmation: *I trust the wisdom of release. I am clearing space for what is true, light, and mine.*

Notes:

____

____

____

____

____

ABOUT THE AUTHOR

Laura Alfano is the visionary behind *Sovereign Living*, a movement to inspire 20 million women worldwide to reclaim their Crown, Heart and Compass, and to fully embody their power. Born and raised in Port Chester, New York, as the eldest of three, she grew up rooted in the values of faith, perseverance, and family. A natural achiever, she graduated high school early, earned her associate's degree in Fashion Merchandising, and went on to complete a bachelor's degree in Marketing and Management at Pace University.

After college, Laura married, welcomed three healthy children into the world, and raised them while simultaneously building a successful career in marketing with leading consumer packaged goods companies and creative agencies in the NY/CT area. She later transitioned into consulting to create a healthier balance for her family, carrying her instinct for beauty and design into every role she touched.

In 2007, Laura's life was forever altered by the sudden loss of her brother. What began in heartbreak set off a chain reaction of deeper pain and disappointment: the unraveling of her marriage and the painful estrangement from two of her children. Following her losses, Laura embarked on a spiritual journey of self-discovery, a season of exploration and awakening. As a devoted student, she traveled widely, studied various yoga lineages, read extensively in the fields of personal growth, and participated in transformational courses. Even an unplanned plant medicine journey became part of her path toward healing. Through this process, Laura reclaimed her Sovereignty, rediscovering her Crown of self-worth, her Heart of compassion, and her Compass of inner wisdom.

Today, Laura lives seaside in Malibu, California, delighting in her role as mother and grandmother. She is a Luxury Real Estate Advisor, a certified Hatha and Kundalini Yoga teacher and Reiki Master. Out of her personal journey, she created the *Sovereign Living* series of books, guided journals, and wisdom cards; resources designed to help women everywhere embody their worth and rise into lives of beauty, balance, joy, and Sovereignty.

DISCOVER THE SOVEREIGN LIVING COLLECTION

Continue your journey of self-discovery and empowerment with the complete *Sovereign Living* series. Alongside each book, you'll find a companion guided journal to help you Reflect, Reframe, and Reconnect, plus a deck of wisdom cards to keep your practice alive every day. Choose one or embrace them all to reclaim your Crown, your Heart, and your Compass.

Sovereign Living I: A Woman's Guide to Reclaiming Your Crown

Sovereign Living I The Sovereign Method:
Reflect • Reframe • Reconnect.
A Guided Journal to Reclaim Your Crown

Sovereign Living I Crown Wisdom Cards:
Daily Guidance to Reclaim Your Crown

Sovereign Living II: A Woman's Guide to Reclaiming Your Heart

Sovereign Living II The Sovereign Method:
Reflect • Reframe • Reconnect.
A Guided Journal to Reclaim Your Heart

Sovereign Living II Heart Wisdom Cards:
Daily Guidance to Reclaim Your Heart

Sovereign Living III: A Woman's Guide to Reclaiming Your Compass

Sovereign Living III The Sovereign Method:
Reflect • Reframe • Reconnect.
A Guided Journal to Reclaim Your Compass

Sovereign Living III Compass Wisdom Cards:
Daily Guidance to Reclaim Your Compass

www.ingramcontent.com/pod-product-compliance
Lightning Source LLC
Chambersburg PA
CBHW071511140726
47997CB00005B/1940